THE BEST OF
ALEXANDER
WHYTE

THE BEST OF
ALEXANDER WHYTE

EDITED BY RALPH G. TURNBULL

BAKER BOOK HOUSE
Grand Rapids, Michigan

Copyright 1953 by
Fleming H. Revell Company

Reprinted 1968 by
Baker Book House Company
with permission of copyright owner
Second printing: September, 1979
ISBN: 0-8010-9628-6

Formerly published under the title,
The Treasury of Alexander Whyte

Printed in the United States of America

Contents

6

Foreword

I COUNT IT a fortunate day that early in my ministry I made the acquaintance of Alexander Whyte, the noted minister of Free St. George's Church, Edinburgh. I met him by way of his volumes of *Bible Characters,* a series of sermons preached to his Sunday evening congregations. I am not sure, but I may have first heard of him before that, through my two older brothers, who spent a graduate year in the New College, Edinburgh, when Dr. Whyte was at the zenith of his power and fame.

He who reads Whyte's *Bible Characters* will be struck, first of all, with the fact that Whyte believed he was a great sinner, and that all men are great sinners, and that the heart is desperately wicked and deceitful above all else. In his chapter on *David and His Vices,* he says: "I am warned of God that with all my study and all my watchfulness and all my prayerfulness, the deceitfulness and the internal hypocrisy of my own heart will still deceive me. Well, all I shall say in answer to that is this—that if my heart is worse than I know it to be, then the God of all grace, with all the blood of His Son, and with all the patience and power of His Spirit, help me."

Another striking thing is Whyte's happy use of illustrations from biographies and autobiographies, formal and informal, such as of Bunyan, St. Theresa, St. Augustine, Thomas Boston, Cardinal Newman; the great Puritan, Goodwin; John Foster, and others.

In his own original way Dr. Whyte is always preaching to his own soul, talking to the souls of others, speaking to Christ, and ever pointing the sinner to Christ on the Cross.

9

Here are some of the passages which I marked in these sermons long ago, and which have a particular message for the preacher:

In the *Sermon on Isaiah:* "Only once did God choose a completely sinless preacher. Always, but that once, God has chosen sinful men, and not seldom the most sinful of men He could get to speak to their fellow men about salvation and sin. . . . It takes a great sinner to preach, as well as to hear, like that. You must call and ordain and inspire a leper if you would have passion in your pulpit like that. And you must be lepers yourselves to put up with passion in your pulpits like that."

In the sermon on *David and His Graces:* "Who is that roaring all day long on the murderous wheel, out of joint, and broken in pieces with the hammer and the anger of God? Do you not know? That is the Prodigal Son of the Old Testament. That is the anointed of the Lord, that is the King of Israel, that is the man after God's own heart."

Again, in the sermon on *David and His Vices:* "Preaching is magnificent work if only we could get preachers like Nathan, if our preachers had only something like Nathan's skill, serpent-like wisdom and evangelical instancy. But even Nathan himself would be helpless with some of you. . . . We ministers must far more study Nathan's method. Nathan's sword was within an inch of the king's conscience before David knew that Nathan had a sword. One sudden thrust, and the king was at Nathan's feet."

In the sermon on *Paul and Felix,* Whyte quotes one whom he calls "the prince of pure and expository preachers"—no doubt Thomas Goodwin: "The Conscience is what the snout is in a bear, a tender part to take him by."

Napoleon once said that "men of imagination rule the world." They rule the pulpit also. Whyte made happy use of imagination. For example, in his sermon on Onesiphorus: "Many were the nights when, after a trying day and then a refreshing supper, Onesiphorus would give out this well selected Psalm at family worship:

> 'Who sow in tears, a reaping time,
> Of joy enjoy they shall' (Psalm 126).

It was of those many Sabbath supper parties that Paul remembered and wrote to Timothy in his Second Epistle to him, "how oft Onesimus refreshed me, and in how many things he ministered to me at Ephesus, thou knowest very well."

And this on *Jacob's Staff:* "That staff, at the first, had been a birthday gift from his twin brother, Esau. When he saw that Jacob envied it, Esau smoothed the stout branch better, and straightened it out and carved E. and J. into a true lover's knot under the handle of it, and laid it beside Jacob's lentil dish on the morning of their double birthday. . . . That staff felt like so much lead when Jacob took it into his hand to run from home; but he would need it, and though it sometimes burned his hand to a red-hot cinder, somehow, he never could throw it away. That staff stood sentinel over its dreaming master at Bethel, and with its help he waded the Jordan and sprang the Jabbok, till he laid it down to water Rachel's sheep in Padan-aram."

In Whyte's volume entitled *With Mercy and With Judgment,* I find the sermon, "The Swelling of the Jordan" (Jeremiah 12:5), well marked. This (in 1917) was the last sermon he preached in St. George's Church. The sermon is altogether biographical, in a devotional sense. Perhaps the preacher knew that the Jordan was not far in front of him. His purpose is to tell what other souls have done in the swelling of the Jordan. First, he speaks of Jesus, His agony in Gethsemane, His prayer on the Cross, "Father into thy hands I commend my spirit." Then the thief on the cross, "Lord, remember me when thou comest into thy kingdom." And then Stephen, "Lord Jesus, receive my spirit. Lay not this sin to their charge." And then Paul, when he went down into the Jordan, "I am ready to be offered, and the time of my departure is at hand." And then St. Augustine, who had one of his students paint the 32nd Psalm on the wall opposite his bed:

> O blessed is the man to whom
> Is freely pardoned
> All the transgression he hath freely done;
> Whose sin is covered.

And then on Luther: "Jesus Christ is my Lord and my God." On Hopeful, in *Pilgrim's Progress:* "Be of good cheer, my brother, for I feel the bottom, and it is good." And then Bishop Butler, who said to his chaplain, "I am still afraid to die." To whom the chaplain said, "My lord, you have forgotten that Jesus Christ is a Saviour. It is written, 'Him that cometh unto me I will in no wise cast out.' " "True," said the Bishop, "and I am surprised; though I have read this Scripture a thousand times over, I never felt its virtue till this moment, and now I die happy."

I know of no one better qualified, by reason of his Scottish background, his Edinburgh training, and his warm evangelical faith, to edit this volume of Dr. Whyte's sermons than Dr. Ralph Turnbull. I feel sure that this collection of Dr. Whyte's writings and sermons will be an important and helpful edition to the library of all preachers whose desire it is to proclaim the "glorious gospel of the blessed God."

CLARENCE E. MACARTNEY.

THE BEST OF
ALEXANDER WHYTE

Whyte of St. George's

THE NEWS of the death of Dr. Alexander Whyte has sent a thrill of sorrow and a sense of impoverishment into every land. Whyte of St. George's—for such was the name which became a household word many years ago—was an extraordinary man, unlike anyone else one ever saw. He was one of the very few men of our generation, or, for that matter, of any other generation, concerning whom every one must agree that they were men of sheer genius. Some such men appear in quiet places, and their genius discovers itself only to one here and there who may chance to push back the leaves and find it in the lowly and concealing grass. Others, of whom he was one, find themselves in positions which proclaim their genius to the ends of the earth, and far and near "stir the great minds of men."

His origin was very humble. He began life as a poor child in Kirriemuir, the Thrums of J. M. Barrie. Through his solitary and precocious childhood he struggled for education and developed his passion for books. Strange and wonderful glimpses of that time we sometimes had from him, as when he told us of the two saints of Kirriemuir. These two villagers were the great lights and high ideals of his childhood, and they represent in a most picturesque fashion the two sides of his own imaginative and religious life. One was, I think, a draper of the typically Calvinistic type produced by the old Scottish theology, and the little child would watch him pacing to and fro on the pavement in front of his shop, with a look of fear and awe on his face and strange words of wrestling on his lips. The other was a different kind of saint, who would knock on Alexander Whyte's window before daybreak on summer mornings, and lead him far into the woods and hills, with a fishing rod in his hand and a short black pipe in his mouth, through the blue smoke of which he would talk all day to the child about religious things, as they fished side by side. When he was quite an old man he still retained the influence of these two, understanding then, what he little dreamed at the time, that they were for him the protagonists of the long battle of his soul, incarnate Hebraism and Hellenism.

In the University of Aberdeen he was one of those who might have stood for George Macdonald's student portraits, in the life which that great Scotsman has made classical and familiar. Through the New College of Edinburgh and onwards by various degrees he worked his way, until he became minister of Free St. George's Church, Edinburgh. Half a century has passed since then, but St. George's, better perhaps than any other place, retains the tradition and heritage of the past. Gone indeed are the lords of session, the statesmen, the writers of books, the leaders of public life in that day, now so dead and so long past. Yet steadily through his whole ministry he drew round him men and women of the same type, and to tell his story would be to write the literary and political history of fifty years.

Very soon it was manifest that St. George's had secured a king of preachers and of men. His pulpit was his throne, from which he ruled a world-wide empire of the mind.

The famous Dr. Candlish, great alike as preacher and ecclesiastic, lay dying in that room in Melville Street which afterward became the study, first of Dr. Whyte, then of Hugh Black, and finally my own. Whyte and Rainy were summoned to the deathbed, and the dying man with characteristic brevity gave them their last charge:

"Rainy, I hand over to you the New College. Whyte, I

had hoped to be your assistant for some years yet, but it is not the will of God. To you I give St. George's. God bless you both! Good-by!"

Such was the charge with which Whyte was left in sole command. And for over twenty years he held the post without assistance. People who did not know thought that a colleagueship with Candlish must be a difficult if not impossible task for any younger man. But Dr. Whyte never found it so, and in the countless times I have heard him speak of his great associate I never heard any word that was not full of both reverence and affection.

He married the daughter of a distinguished Scotch family, and seven children grew up around them. Their home was the center and gathering-place of notable men and women from every part of the world. There you would meet leaders in politics, special movements, art, science, and literature—the Bab from Mt. Carmel, and this or that Maharajah from India, lords of literature, and leaders of religion from America and from every land of Europe.

He was loyal to his church, and became a sort of center of the ecclesiastical life and controversies of his times. Yet more and more he shrank back from taking any active part in them, until in latter days you saw his figure silent, sphinxlike, with those beautiful and massive features of his crowned by their white locks of hair, expressing no opinion, committing himself to no party, thinking his own thoughts, in silence and in mystery. And yet every man in the mêlée felt his presence there, restraining controversy from unbecoming words, and tempering the mood of debate with the serenity of another world. It is difficult for ordinary mortals to say all that unsanctified human nature desires to say in the immediate presence of the saints.

In 1909 he was offered the principalship of the New College on the death of Dr. Marcus Dods. This office he put from him resolutely, and refused to discuss the arguments that his friends would fain have brought to bear when they sought to induce him to accept it. But that summer, having gone to the hills around St. Mary's Loch, something happened. He never would explain it. Perhaps he never could. It was some sort of a mystic vision in which he heard the Lord manifestly speaking to him. At all events, he returned to Edinburgh, took up the burden, and filled the office with memorable distinction.

In what was known as the Great Church Case Dr. Whyte was a kind of central point round which as a spiritual standard the United Free Church gathered. The case is well known. It was one in which the property of the United Free Church was claimed by a small fraction of the old Free Church of Scotland on the ground that the union between that church and the United Presbyterian Church had been illegal from the point of view of ancient title deeds. Dr. Whyte went up to London and watched assiduously the final trial through all its stages in the House of Lords, where it was tried by seven judges. When he came back I asked him his impression, and he said to me, in that Johnsonian, epigrammatic way of his:

"Sir, I saw seven men standing on their trial and being judged!"

When the great war broke out his four sons all volunteered for service, and one of them fell at Loos. At a meeting where we both spoke not long afterward, I heard him refer to the fact that all his children were serving in the war, and he added:

"If I had twenty of them I would give them all."

When in 1916 I was able to go out at last among the fighting men, it was at a time when our policy was more and more to relieve his failing strength and to allow me to take the heavier parts of the work. But on the emergency he at once stepped forward and shouldered the burdens appropriate to a younger man. He had enormous physical strength, and his physique had always been robust and apparently untirable. Somehow, in the day of dire need people forgot his eighty years, and it surprised no one to see him breasting into the battle with amazing and unquenchable energy.

His whole soul was in the negotiations for union with the Established Church of Scotland. In that matter also he was for the most part a silent witness, but he never, to my knowledge, missed a single meeting of the committees, and there, as in all other affairs, his presence acted with the force of restraining grace, and kept men's consciences up to their highest levels.

He was shy, and most of those who knew him felt a certain aloofness and tenderness of sympathy. For their affairs he had the openest of hearts, but he seldom spoke of his own most intimate concerns. It is characteristic of many Scotsmen that the doors of their hearts open only for the coming in of friends, very rarely for the letting out of confidences. Yet no man was more friendly than he, nor rejoiced more in banding himself with kindred spirits. There was an innermost circle which for many years made a kind of palladium in his life, and into that circle few indeed were admitted. Henry Drummond had been in long ago— Webster Thompson, Marcus Dods, Taylor Innes, and John Sutherland Black. He alone of all the band remains alive today, the rest are united on the other side. Would that we might have record of their conferences as they walked out or sat in that great study in Charlotte Square, discussing all matters of the hour or of the past, or playfully rallying each other on the individual parts they played on the great stage! As they left him he became more and more solitary, and we of a younger generation who were privileged by our work to have very intimate contact with him received more and more the confidence of a lonely man whose friends of the older generation had mostly passed away.

We would have laid down our lives for him, Hugh Black and I. The only difference we ever had with him was that by all sorts of subtle ways he thrust us forward into any prominent or desirable position which he himself was expected to take, and we had to watch him for this, and circumvent his too great generosity. Generous he was, almost to a fault, judging everybody, worthy or unworthy, by the standards of his own kind heart rather than by the achievements of his friend, and rejoicing always in the success of those he loved more than in his own. When we listened to his long confessions of the general depravity of the ministerial mind, and especially of his own malice and envy and jealousy toward his truest friends, we simply laughed, knowing better. So far did this extend that there was no possibility of winning his favor by following in his lines. In the vestry, after one had preached, he almost always had some kind thing to say, and in the strength of a couple of sentences we went out into the street taller and more erect and feeling that life was worth living when a man like him should speak that way to one of us. But I remember well on one occasion, under the sense that my own preaching had been of recent Sundays rather far removed from his region, trying to speak through an afternoon service in his own vein. All that he said to me afterward in the vestry was:

"Deliver your own message."

And from that day forth I have tried to deliver it.

In later years his health began to fail, but he persistently demanded that he should be permitted to die in harness.

On one occasion he intimated this to the congregation, and nearly broke the hearts of some of his friends by announcing that his choice was to die on the doorstep of some of the aged saints of St. George's. At last, however, he was persuaded to retire to a village in the south of England, where he took surreptitious opportunities of addressing the villagers in the local congregation on such themes as the teaching of John Bunyan. He was a great expositor of Bunyan, and I recollect that on one occasion when I was staying in the neighborhood of Bedford and visiting the scenes depicted in *Pilgrim's Progress* or connected with the life of John Bunyan, I found over the mantelpiece of a cottager there a framed portrait of Dr. Whyte. Later the family moved to London, where they occupied a house in Hampstead, which became a rendezvous of old friends and a place of pilgrimage for people of all the world. It was there that he passed peacefully away in his sleep on the night of Friday, the 7th of January, 1921.

He might have had a great career as a politician, or as an actor, for he had quite exceptional dramatic power. His position among writers is a distinguished one, but, after all, his writings were simply printed preaching, and it was as a preacher that he attained to his greatest eminence. Those, however, who knew him most intimately will not hesitate to add that he was greatest of all as a man and as a friend.

Everybody who knew him was impressed with the vast extent and accuracy of his knowledge of books. Sometimes he struck you as a lover of books, and sometimes as a kind of intellectual beast of prey who sprang on a book and tore it to pieces and knew the heart of it in one swift act of appropriation. For many years he seemed to read everything that was published. I remember one evening when some of his friends congratulated him on the long row of books wet from the printer that were waiting for him on his study shelf, and he replied:

"That's nothing! That's nothing, sir!"

Yet with all his voracious appetite for reading the home of his intellect was ever in the Bible. He would end a letter with a couple of texts, or send a post card half across the world with one reference and his initials. Next after the Bible came the Puritans and the Covenanters. Goodwin was his special favorite, and he would tell us how his Goodwin "fell out of his boards, and I bound him in morocco." In Bunyan and all that concerned him he moved as in his home fields, while Jonathan Edwards and many another of the highest lights of those days were his familiar friends. Everybody knows how he sought out and brought to light obscure persons of that ilk, such as Fraser of Brea and Thomas Shepard of Boston. These and their associates had lain so long in the outer darkness of oblivion that they always seemed to be blinking in the sunlight into which he brought them. And, indeed, there is no doubt that many of them had reason to do so, for while Dr. Whyte never missed real greatness where it was, he frequently discovered it where it was not. And some of these Puritans used to provoke his congregations to a constant feeling that they were, both in intellectual and religious quality, very far behind him who had resurrected them, and who was now sitting at their feet.

Other writers, both old and new, came in abundance at his call. He may be said to have created the modern Scottish type of Bible class, which superseded the old catechizing one. Going forth for the sake of his pupils among the great fields of old and new times, he brought home much prey. Dante, Cicero and Marcus Aurelius, Thackeray, Tennyson and Rudyard Kipling, Hermann of Marburg and Sabatier, all fell to his bow. Wherever there was a great mind anywhere it had for him a singular attraction. For years after Dr. Dods died I was joint editor with him of the Bible Class Handbooks, and our work in that connection was to me a liberal education. While he himself wrote on the Shorter Catechism, he would welcome writing that was vital on any subject whatsoever, and was altogether a great humorist. I know no word which so well expresses him as the word which he himself almost invented, "appreciator." Walter Pater had published his book under the well-known title of *Appreciations*. Whether that had anything to do with his appropriating the term I know not. Certain it is that no man living or dead could better claim the word. He had had from his birth a literary taste and instinct which gave a high distinction to his prayers and to his sermons, but he was always enriching it by some newly found word or phrase. Roget's *Thesaurus* was constantly at his elbow, as he would say.

He could not sing a note, yet his mind was perpetually caught in the rhymed meshes of favorite hymns, and no one can think of him for long without finding himself lilting a few familiar words, such as:

> Direct, control, suggest this day
> Whate'er I think, or do, or say.
>
> O, may we stand before the Lamb
> When earth and seas are fled.

Those of us who wanted his matchless exposition of Scripture found that we had a hard task to keep him from preaching continually on hymns. The sermons on "Just As I Am" were among the most famous of these utterances. He would read the hymn from beginning to end, and comment on it almost word for word, and no one who heard them has forgotten the vivid power of these comments.

"Just as I am, poor, wretched, blind, sight, riches, healing of the mind. . . . Healing of the mind! Do you remember Hamlet, 'Canst thou not minister to a mind diseased?' Healing of the mind, sir!"

The old Scottish Psalms, however, surpassed any of the hymns in his affections. Even into his prayers they entered, and many a funeral prayer and address have ended in one of them. In funeral services he was in his most familiar mood, and often broke into verse. His part, for instance, in Henry Drummond's funeral was almost entirely occupied by the quotation of the two lines:

> When the shore is reached at last,
> Who will count the billows past?

He had an ear for literature which gave great distinction to his own expressions. He was attracted to characteristic words, which he used with such power that those who heard him speak them can hear that sound again whenever they meet the word. This catholic delight in books and thought led him far afield. Newman and Martineau were equally welcome when either of them brought some living truth in his hand. Distinctions between things secular and sacred disappeared at his touch. I well remember one conversation about books, in which I sat between him and Alexander McLaren of Manchester, who that day had honored me with his presence—I think on the last occasion on which he went out to lunch. I had asked only Dr. Whyte to meet him, and the two sat there, lionlike old men, and went over the heaps of spoil and the mountains of prey that they had devoured during their long and wonderful lifetimes.

Yet there can be no doubt as to where Dr. Whyte's essential place was. He has been called the last of the Puritans, and the name is a happy one. He always gravitated toward conscience, or else soared automatically toward the regions of mysticism, and the combination of conscience with mysticism gives an analysis of the Puritan spirit than which none could be more complete. William Law, Jacob Boehme, and anybody else who was a master in these regions, was a friend of Dr. Whyte's. And in later days, after the wide wanderings which already have been referred to, he came back to them as to his spirit's home. One summer very near the end of his ministry he was packing his portmanteau with books for his country reading, and I, who had been fascinated by Francis Thompson and his "Hound of Heaven," besought him to add this to his summer's reading, and accept my copy. He did so, and when he returned after some months to Edinburgh I asked him how he had liked the volume. With a curious half-ashamed and half-exultant glance he said to me that he was sorry he had never read it. The fact was he had put eleven volumes of Thomas Shepard into the portmanteau, and had never got at it!

He was a Puritan risen from the dead, and prophesying in pagan times to a later generation. He was Faithful in Vanity Fair, without the incident of the martyrdom. His spirit was two hundred years old, yet it remained fresh as the spirit of a little child.

During the younger days and well on into the middle time he was known throughout the land as par excellence the prophet of sin. Nobody doubted his prophetic authority. The preacher's business is the transmission of personality laden with truth. Dr. Whyte had from first to last an overwhelming sense of the greatness of the pulpit, and in talking to young aspirants to the ministry I have heard him many times advise them to neglect any part of their work rather than the preparation for the pulpit. In the pulpit he was a man of passion. Nobody ever heard from his lips any cold truth. He was never ashamed of getting into a state. His passion ran easily into wildness, and it was from him that one learned that a certain amount of wildness and capacity for it is an absolute necessity for all effective preaching.

Of course, this temperament is dangerous, and a man who lets it go free is apt to make a fool of himself. But that would never have concerned Dr. Whyte. He was hopeless for literalists. They called him exaggerated, and one-sided, and many other adjectives of the same kind, but he hit even his critics, and left the arrow quivering in their flesh. His preaching was hot truth let loose, and one hearing him many a time remembered the words of Jesus: "I am come to send fire on the earth." So utterly did he commit himself to the Spirit of the Lord when he opened his mouth and taught that he gave to many of us the impression that a man will never go so far in the real progress either of thought or of utterance as when he knows not whither he is going.

Like his own John Bunyan, his basis was experience. He preached nothing beyond the terrors and the glories among which his own heart had trembled or rejoiced. He was intensely personal, and had no use for abstractions of any kind. He spoke no generalities, and was always thinking of living men and women. Apparently the simplest of men, he was yet also the shrewdest in his judgments, and you took your life in your hand when you went to hear him preach. In this modern world, so fond of polite generalities, so drugged with phrases, he cut to the bone of sheer reality. His Old Testament and New Testament characters lived and walked the streets of Edinburgh in glory and in shame, and the Edinburgh people discovered that it was themselves he was talking about under ancient Hebrew names.

His sense of sin was crushing. Sometimes it was terrifying almost to madness. Under all his music there was the deep vibrating tone of it, like the undertones of a great organ. He had no respect whatever for those who thought lightly of sin. One day he had been giving a lamentable account of Thomas Shepard's jealousy of a friend who had preached for him, describing how he turned his face to the wall when he heard his wife's favorable report of the preacher, and so on at considerable length. A friend went into the vestry afterward, and, greatly daring, said to him: "Doctor, that man you were talking about today had nothing wrong with his soul. He should have sent for a doctor, and got his body put right. Evidently his liver was out of order."

The keen eyes twinkled as he laid his hand on his friend's shoulder, and said: "My dear fellow, you haven't any knowledge whatsoever of the black depths of the human heart!"

But the most merciless attack on the man of light mind was his treatment of the rich young ruler. Him he hated in the name of the Lord. He described in most amazing terms his immaculate babyhood, boyhood and youth, ran him along his career until at last he died, watched him and made his congregation see him wheeling blindly down the black depths of the inferno, circle after circle, until just as he disappeared on his way down its bottomless abyss, he, who had been bending over the pulpit, watching him with blazing eyes, shouted: "I hear it! It's the mocking laughter of the universe, and it's shouting at him over the edge, 'Ha, ha! Kept the commandments!'"

Like John Bunyan of old, he "feared nothing and said anything" with a courage that made your heart stand still as he preached. Many incidents of this might be adduced, and everyone who writes on him will have something else of the kind to say. The famous passage of the hellhounds is perhaps the best known, in which he tells of a man who has sinned and who is now the victim of remorse. God sets His hellhounds on him, and you see the man shivering under his blankets as he hears them baying while he tries to sleep in his bed at night, and so on you follow this ghastly chase until at last he dies.

"You may be saved," shouted the preacher, "but they will follow you up to the very gates of heaven, and leave their marks on the golden bars."

So he scourged the good easy men and women of his times and the fashionable life of his land. Some who preferred smoother words blamed him for this, and did not know the power and the bite of it on those more sorely tempted.

He was preaching once on "If I make my bed in hell." The gist of the sermon was that if you make your bed in hell you will have to lie on it. Walking homeward from the Assembly Hall, in which the address had been given, along the dark wintry streets of Edinburgh, just as he was passing the end of one of those streets that enter Princes Street from the north, a cloaked figure sprang out on him and seized his arm. A voice whispered hoarsely, "I've made my bed in hell," and the man vanished into the night.

One of the leading business men of Scotland, whose honorable career alike in church and state was known to a wide circle in and beyond the land, told me that it was these sermons that kept him from desperate temptations, and had set his feet on those rocks of faith whereon he had been able to stand through a difficult lifetime.

Yet, with all this, there was never any arrogance or sense of superiority. His fiercest accusations were always against himself. On one occasion, when a prominent citizen had been imprisoned, and the whole city was aghast at the scandal, as Dr. Whyte came into the vestry on Sunday morning the bells were ringing for church. He turned to me and said: "Do you hear those bells? He hears them in his prison cell this morning. Man, it might have been me!"

To the great astonishment and even (I fear) to the amusement of those of us who had reason to know his boundless generosity, both of judgment and of heart, he had a way of accusing himself of all imaginable ministerial iniquities, such as malice and envy and jealousy and the like. On one occasion, down in a drunken slum, he astonished his audience by informing them that he had found out the name of the wickedest man in Edinburgh, and he had come to tell them; and bending forward he whispered: "His name is Alexander Whyte."

In these moods, standing face to face with the tragedy of sin, with himself and all his world at the bar of conscience, he would come forth with an expression on his face that was the most uncanny thing I ever witnessed. We were afraid as we looked on him, and when after some terrific denunciation he would shut his mouth and look abroad on the people, every one of us felt as if it were the day of judgment.

Yet, on the other hand, he was a man of the most tender humanity, and he had an immense compassion. The combination of this with the power of his other self used to remind one of the couplet in Browning:

> As one spring wind unbinds the mountain snows
> And comforts violets in their hermitage.

Sensitive and proud he was, yet always friendly, and his reticence made him all the more wonderful when he opened his heart to a friend. While he denounced men in the mass and attacked them savagely in groups, no man ever lived who was more tender and kindly in his private judgments, or more averse to wounding the sensibilities of a friend. One poor old woman whom he visited had complained during the whole of twenty minutes about everybody and everything, and he had sat silent. Then he lifted his gloves and hat, and shook hands with her to bid her good-by, saying only: "And mind you forget not all His benefits!"

On another occasion, visiting one who had more cause for complaint, and whose heart was well-nigh broken, he kneeled down with her in her poor room, and said simply: "O Lord, here's two poor old folk needing you sorely. You won't be hard on us!"

The most distinctive feature of his later life was its growing spirituality. The last phase of it was marked by a serenity and vision which were very wonderful. The long years of repression and discipline had left him the most thoroughly spiritually exercised man I ever knew. But now he had attained to be an expert believer, and he bore no sign of the struggles of past years. Now he met all events with the tenderest gentleness and compassion. His one great exercise was the practice of the presence of God, and he walked with Christ every day. His prayers retained the echo of the great wrestlings of former days. "What is His name?" he would burst out at the beginning of a prayer, "what is His name, and what is His Son's name? Who is a God like unto Thee?" It was not sin now, but the forgiveness of sin, and the victory over it, and the promise of holiness, that we got from him. And when he thought of death the words that continually sprang to his lips were, "The souls of believers are at their death made perfect in holiness, and pass immediately into glory."

He was a man obviously saved by the recurring surprise and daily wonder of Christ. He found many around him taking Christ for granted, and heeding Him very little. But to him Christ came with a new astonishment every morning, with a new amazement of love and grace every evening. The sacraments became more and more precious to him. They were the great events of the year, and he journeyed from one of them to the next as a man counts landmarks on his pilgrimage. In them he rose above the earth altogether. They were genuine banquets of the spirit, symposia where men ate and drank at the table of God, places for conversation between the soul and Christ, where all that his life had strained after and his faith had laid hold on became the actual and present reality.

One of the most strongly marked features of this period was the growing exhilaration with which he thought about death. When Dr. Marcus Dods died Dr. Whyte preached his funeral sermon in St. George's. From beginning to end it was a kind of shout of triumph. It began with the astonishing sentence, "I always thought that Marcus would be preaching my funeral sermon, and here's me preaching his." And in the same strain it went on, following further than it is usually given the eyes of friends to follow their beloved. Yet all that he said was convincing, and we felt that his excursions into the world to come were no words of imagination or of fancy, but were simply records of things that he had seen and heard. His favorite quotation in those days was that already referred to:

> O, may we stand before the Lamb
> When earth and seas are fled,
> And hear the Judge pronounce our name
> With blessings on our head.

Yet to the end he never could forget those who were caring for none of these things. He remembered them even when looking out over the gold bar of heaven, and many a time in spirit

> He laid his face between his hands and wept.
> We heard his tears.

"What will it be to be there?" he would cry at the close of such a sermon. Then he would add: "Aye, and what will it be not to be there?"

He is there, and, for my part, with eyes and heart and memory and great love I follow him very wistfully. What must it be to be in Alexander Whyte's heaven?

The Magnificence of Prayer

Lord, teach us to pray.
LUKE 11:1.
A royal priesthood.
I PETER 2:9.

"I AM an apostle," said Paul; "I magnify mine office." And we also have an office. Our office is not the apostolic office, but Paul would be the first to say to us that our office is quite as magnificent as ever his office was. Let us, then, magnify our office. Let us magnify its magnificent opportunities, its momentous duties, and its incalculable and everlasting rewards. For our office is the "royal priesthood." And we do not nearly enough magnify and exalt our royal priesthood. To be "kings and priests unto God"—what a magnificent office is that! But, then, we who hold that office are men of such small and such mean minds, our souls so decline and so cleave to this earth, that we never so much as attempt to rise to the height and the splendor of our magnificent office. If our minds were only enlarged and exalted at all up to our office, we would be found of God far oftener than we are, with our scepter in our hand, and with our miter on our head. If we magnified our office as Paul magnified his office we would achieve as magnificent results in our office as ever he achieved in his. The truth is, Paul's mannificent results were achieved more in our office than in his own. It was because Paul added the royal priesthood to the Gentile apostleship that he achieved such magnificent results in that apostleship. And if we would but magnify our royal priesthood as Paul did—it hath not entered into our hearts so much as to conceive what God hath prepared for those who properly perform their office as kings and priests unto God.

Prayer is the magnificent office it is because it is an office of such a magnificent kind. Magnificence is of many kinds, and magnificent things are more or less magnificent according to their kind. This great globe on which it strikes its roots and grows is magnificent in size when compared with that grain of mustard seed; but just because that grain of mustard seed is a seed and grows, that smallest of seeds is far greater than the great globe itself. A bird on its summer branch is far greater than the great sun in whose warmth he builds and sings, because that bird has life and love and song, which the sun, with all its immensity of size and with all its light and heat, has not. A cup of cold water only, given to one of these little ones in the name of a disciple, is a far greater offering before God than thousands of rams and ten thousands of rivers of oil, because there is charity in that cup of cold water. And an ejaculation, a sigh, a sob, a tear, a smile, a psalm, is far greater to God than all the oblations, and incense, and new moons, and Sabbaths, and calling of assemblies, and solemn meetings of Jerusalem, because repentance and faith and love and trust are in that sob and in that psalm. And the magnificence of all true prayer —its nobility, its royalty, its absolute divinity—all stand in this, that it is the greatest kind of act and office that man or angel can ever enter on and perform. Earth is at its very best, and heaven is at its very highest, when men and angels magnify their office of prayer and of praise before the throne of God.

1. The magnificence of God is the source and the measure of the magnificence of prayer. "Think magnificently of God," said Paternus to his son. Now, that counsel is the sum and substance of this whole matter. For the heaven and the

earth, the sun and the moon and the stars, the whole opening universe of our day, the Scriptures of truth, with all that
they contain; the Church of Christ, with all her services and
all her saints—all are set before us to teach us and to compel
us indeed to "think magnificently of God." And they have
all fulfilled the office of their creation when they have all
combined to make us think magnificently of their Maker.
Consider the heavens, the work of His fingers, the moon
and the stars, which He hath ordained: consider the intellectual heavens also, angels and archangels, cherubim and
seraphim; consider mankind also, made in the image of
God; consider Jesus Christ, the express image of His person; consider a past eternity and a coming eternity, and the
revelation thereof that is made to us in the Word of God
and in the hearts of His people—and I defy you to think otherwise than magnificently of God. And, then, after all that,
I equally defy you to forget, or neglect, or restrain prayer.
Once you begin to think aright of Him who is the Hearer
of prayer, and who waits, in all His magnificence, to be gracious to you—I absolutely defy you to live any longer the
life you now live. "First of all, my child," said Paternus to
his son, "think magnificently of God. Magnify His providence: adore His power: frequent His service; and pray to
Him frequently and instantly. Bear Him always in your
mind: teach your thoughts to reverence Him in every place,
for there is no place where He is not. Therefore, my child,
fear and worship, and love God; first and last, think magnificently of God."

2. "Why has God established prayer?" asks Pascal. And
Pascal's first answer to his own great question is this. God
has established prayer in the moral world in order "to com-
municate to His creatures the dignity of causality." That is
to say, to give us a touch and a taste of what it is to be a Creator. But, then, "there are some things ultimate and incausable," says Bacon, that interpreter of nature. And what-

ever things are indeed ultimate to us, and incausable by us, them God "hath put in His own power." But there are many other things, and things that far more concern us, that He communicates to us to have a hand of cause and creation in. Not immediately, and at our own rash and hot hand, and at our precipitate and importunate will, but always under His Holy Hand, and under the tranquillity of His Holy Will. We hold our office and dignity of causality and creation under the Son, just as He holds His under the Father. But, instead of that lessening our dignity, to us, it rather ennobles and endears our dignity. All believers are agreed that they would rather hold their righteousness of Christ than of themselves, and so would all praying men. They would rather that all things had their spring and rise and rule in the wisdom and the love and the power of God than in their own wisdom and love and power, even if they had the wisdom and the love and the power for such an office. But, then, again, just as all believing men put on Jesus Christ to justification of life, so do they all put on, under Him, their royal robe and their priestly diadem and breastplate. And that, not as so many beautiful ornaments, beautiful as they are, but as instruments and engines of divine power. "Thus saith the Lord, the Holy One of Israel," as He clothes His priests with salvation, "Ask me of things to come concerning my sons, and concerning the work of my hands command ye me."

What a thing for God to say to man! What a magnificent office! What a more than royal dignity! What a gracious command, and what a sure encouragement is that to pray! For ourselves, first, as His sons—if His prodigal and dishonorable sons—and then for our fellows, even if they are as prodigal and as undeserving as we are. Ask of me! Even when a father is wounded and offended by his son, even then, you feel sure that you have his heartstrings in your hand when you go to ask him for things that concern his son, and that even though he is a bad son, even when he sends you away in anger, his fatherly bowels move over you as you depart, and he looks out at his door to see if you are coming back to ask him again concerning his son. And when you take boldness and venture back, he falls on your neck and says, Command me all that is in your heart concerning my son. Now, that is the "dignity of causality," that in which you are the cause of a father taking home again his son, and the cause of a son saying, I will arise and go to my father. That is your "magnificent office." That is your "royal priesthood."

3. And then there is this magnificent and right noble thing in prayer. Oh, what a noble God we have! says Pascal —that God shares His creatorship with us! And I will, to the praise and the glory of God this day add this, that He makes us the architects of our own estates and the fashioners of our own fortunes. It is good enough to have an estate left us in this life if we forget we have it; it is good enough that we inherit a fortune in this world's goods if it is not our lasting loss. Only there is nothing great, nothing noble, nothing magnanimous or magnificent in that. But to have begun life with nothing, and to have climbed up by pure virtue, by labor, and by self-denial, and by perseverance, to the very top—this world has no better praise to give her best sons than that. But there is another and a better world, of which this world at its best is but the scaffolding, the preparation, and the porch; and to be the architect of our own fortune in *that* world will be to our everlasting honor.

Now, there is this magnificence about the world of prayer, that in it we work out, not our own bare and naked and "scarce" salvation only, but our everlasting inheritance, incorruptible and undefilable, with all its unsearchable riches. Heaven and earth, time and eternity, creation and providence, grace and glory, are all laid up in Christ; and then Christ and all His unsearchable riches are laid open to prayer, and then it is said to every one of us, Choose you all what you will have, and command me for it! All God's grace and all His truth have been coined—as Goodwin has it—out of purposes into promises; and then all those promises are made "Yea and amen" in Christ, and then out of Christ they are published abroad to all men in the word of the Gospel; and then all men who read and hear the Gospel are put on their mettle. For what a man loves, that that man is. What a man chooses out of a hundred offers, you are sure by that who and what that man is. And, accordingly, put the New Testament in any man's hand, and set the Throne of Grace wide open before any man, and you need no omniscience to tell you that man's true value. If he lets his Bible lie unopened and unread, if he lets God's Throne of Grace stand till death, idle and unwanted, if the depth and the height, the nobleness and the magnificence, the goodness and the beauty of divine things have no command over him, and no attraction to him—then, you do not wish me to put words on the meanness of that man's mind. Look yourselves at what he has chosen, look and weep at what he has neglected and has for ever lost!

But there are other men, there are men of a far nobler blood than that man is; there are great men, royal men; there are some men made of noble stuff and cast into a noble mold. And you will never satisfy or quiet those men with all you can promise them or pour out on them in this life. They are men of a magnificent heart, and only in prayer have their hearts ever got full scope and a proper atmosphere. They would die if they did not pray. They magnify their office. You cannot please them better than to invite and ask them to go to their God in your behalf. They would go of their own motion and accord for you, even if you never asked them. They have prayed for you before you asked them, more than you know. They are like Jesus Christ in this, and He will acknowledge them in this. While you were yet their enemies, they prayed for you and as good as died for you. And when you turn to be their enemies again, they will have their revenge on you at the mercy seat. When you feel, somehow, as if coals of fire were—from somewhere—being heaped on your head, it is from the mercy seat, where that magnanimous man is retaliating on you. Now, not Paul himself ever magnified his office more or better than that. And it was in that very same way that our Lord magnified His royal priesthood when He had on His crown of thorns on the cross, and when His shame covered Him as a robe and a diadem in the sight of God, and when He interceded and said, "They know not what they do."

4. And then there is this fine and noble thing about prayer also, that the acceptableness of it and the power of it are in direct proportion to the secrecy and the spirituality of it. As its stealth is, as its silence is, as its hiddenness away with God is, as its unsuspectedness and undeservedness with men are, as its pure goodness, pure love, and pure good will are, so does prayer perform its magnificent part when it is alone with God. The true closet of the true saint of God is not built of stone and lime. The secret place of God and His people is not a thing of wood and iron, and bolts and bars.

At the same time, Christ did say, *Shut your door*. And in order to have the Holy Ghost, the man after God's own heart in prayer always, as a matter of fact, builds for himself a little sanctuary, all his own, not to shut God in, but to shut all that is not of God out. He builds a house for God before he has as yet built a house for himself. You would not believe it about that man of secret prayer. When you see and hear him, he is the poorest, the meekest, the most contrite, and the most silent of men, and you rebuke him because he so trembles at God's word. If you could but see him when he is alone with the King, if you could but see his nearness and his boldness, you would think that he and the King's Son had been born and brought up together, such intimacies and such passwords are exchanged between

them. You would wonder, you would not believe your eyes
and your ears. If you saw him on his knees you would see a
sight. Look, he is in the Audience Chamber! Look, he is in
the Council Chamber now! He has a seat set for him among
the peers. He is set down among the old nobility of the Empire. The King will not put on His signet ring to seal a
command till your friend has been heard. "Command me,"
the King says to him. "Ask me," He says, "for the things of
my sons: command me things to come concerning them."
And, as if that were not enough, that man of all-prayer is
still on his knees. He is "wrestling" on his knees. There is
no enemy there that I can see. There is nothing and no one
that I can see near him, and yet he wrestles like a mighty
man. What is he doing with such a struggle? Doing? Do
you not know what he is doing? He is moving heaven and
earth. The man is removing mountains. He is casting this
mountain and that into the midst of the sea. He is casting
down thrones. He is smiting old empires of time to pieces.
Yes, he is wrestling indeed! For he is wrestling now with
God, and now with man, now with death, and now with
hell. See, the day breaks over his place of prayer! See, the
Kingdom of God begins to come in on the earth! What a
spot is that! What plots are hatched there! What conspira-
cies are planned there! How dreadful is this place! Let us escape for our life out of it! Is that man, in there with God,
your friend? Can you trust him with God? Will he speak
about you when he is in audience? And what will he say?
Has he anything against you? Have you anything on your
conscience, or in your heart, against him? Then I would
not be you for a world!

But, no, hear him! What is that he says? I declare I hear
your name, and your children's names! And the King
stretches forth His scepter, and your friend touches it. He has
"commanded" his God for you. He has "asked concerning"
you and your sons. Such access, such liberty, such power, such

prevalency, such a magnificent office has he who has been made of God a king and a priest unto God.

5. And then, to cap and to crown it all, the supreme magnanimity and the superb generosity of God to its top perfection are seen in this—in the men He selects, prepares for Himself, calls, consecrates, and clothes with the miter and with the ephod and with the breastplate. It is told in the Old Testament to the blame of Jeroboam, that "he made an house of high places, and made priests of the lowest of the people, which were not of the sons of Levi." But what is written and read in the Levitical law to Jeroboam's blame, that very same thing, and in these very same words, God's saints are this Sabbath day singing in their thousands to His praise before the throne of God and the Lamb. For, ever since the day of Christ, it has been the lowest of the people —those lowest, that is, in other men's eyes, and in their own—it has been the poor and the despised, and the meek, and the hidden, and the downtrodden, and the silent, who have had secret power and privilege with God, and have prevailed. It was so, sometimes, even in the Old Testament. The New Testament sometimes broke up through the Old, and in nothing more than in this in the men—and in their mothers—who were made kings and priests unto God. "The Lord maketh poor," sang Samuel's mother, "and maketh rich: he bringeth low, and lifteth up. He raiseth up the poor out of the dust, and lifteth up the beggar from the dunghill, to set them among princes, and to make them inherit the throne of glory." And the mother of our great High Priest Himself sang, as she sat over His manger, "He hath regarded the low estate of his handmaiden. . . . He hath filled the hungry with good things; and the rich hath he sent empty away." This, then, is the very topmost glory and the very supremest praise of God—the men, from among men, that He takes, and makes of them kings and priests unto God. Let all such men magnify their office.

Imagination in Prayer

Lord, teach us to pray.
LUKE 11: 1.

Full of eyes.
REVELATION 4: 8.

I NEVER SEE, or hear, or speak, or write the word "imagination" without being arrested and recalled to what Pascal and Butler and Edwards have all said, with such power and with such passion, on the subject of imagination. Pascal—himself all compact of imagination as he is—sets forth again and again a tremendous indictment against the "deceits" and "deceptions" of the imagination. Butler also, in few but always weighty words, stigmatizes the imagination as "that forward and delusive faculty," while Jonathan Edwards, in his own masterful way, would almost seem to have given the death blow to the use of the imagination in all matters of personal and experimental religion. But as to Butler, that great author's latest and best editor, in two paragraphs of really fine criticism, has clearly brought out that what Butler calls "the errors of the imagination" are not errors of the imagination at all, but are the errors of unbridled fancy and caprice, and of an unbalanced and ill-regulated judgment. "It seems probable," so sums up Butler's venerable editor, "that this is one of the rare instances in which Butler, relaxing the firmness of his hold, forgets himself, and assumes a licence in the use of words." And then the editor turns the tables on his admired author by going on to say that, in felicity of imaginative illustration,

Butler is the equal of Macaulay himself, while, in some other of the exercises of the imagination, Butler is even above Burke.

What, then, you will ask—with all that—what exactly, and in itself, and at its best, is the *imagination?* Well, come back for a moment to the very beginning of all things if you would have the best answer to the question. And then I will answer that question by asking and answering another: "How did God create man?" "God created man," I am answered, "male and female, after his own *image,* in knowledge, righteousness, and holiness, with dominion over the creatures." Our understanding, then, our mind and our memory, are all so many images to us of the Divine Mind. Our conscience, again, is an inward voice to us, impressing on us an imprint of the Divine Righteousness and the Divine Law. Our will, also, and the Divine Will, are of the same Divine Substance. And as for our heart, it is "a copy, Lord, of Thine." And, then, in his *imagination,* man possesses, and exercises in himself, a certain, and that a not very far-off, likeness of the Divine Omnipresence and the Divine Omniscience. For, by his imagination, a man can look behind, and before, and around, and within, and above. By his imagination a man can go back to the beginning ere ever the earth was. One man has done it. Moses has done it. And what Moses has done to this earth—that one day will not be remembered nor come into mind—all that, John, Moses' fellow in imagination, has done to the new heaven and the new earth. The imagination, then, whatever else it is, is not that "forward, ever-intruding and delusive faculty": it is not that "author of all error," as Butler, so unlike himself, so confuses and miscalls it. Nor is it what Pascal so lashes to death with his splendid invective. Nor is it imagination at all, as we have to do with it today, that Edwards so denounces in his *Religious Affections.*

Imagination, as God in His goodness gave it at first to

man—imagination is nothing less than the noblest intellectual attribute of the human mind. And his imagination is far more to every spiritually minded man than a merely intellectual attribute of his mind. I shall not need to go beyond Pascal himself, so splendidly endowed with this splendid gift. "Imagination," says Pascal, "creates all the beauty, and all the justice, and all the happiness that is in the heart of man." The imagination, then, must not be made to bear the blame that really belongs to those men who have prostituted it, and have filled its great inward eyes full of visions of folly and sin, when they should have set the Lord always before their inward eyes, with all His works in nature and in grace and in glory. Because there is only one of a city, and two of a family, who ever employ their inward eyes aright, are the inward eyes of those men to be plucked out who have on their inward eyes an unction from the Holy One? No, a thousand times, no! "Open thou mine eyes, that I may behold wondrous things out of thy law. I am a stranger in the earth: hide not thy commandments from me."

If, then, you would learn to pray to perfection, that is to say, to pray with all that is within you, never fail, never neglect, to do this. Never once shut your bodily eyes and bow your knees to begin to pray, without, at the same moment, opening the eyes of your imagination. It is but a bodily service to shut our outward eyes and not at the same moment open the eyes of our inner man. Do things like this, then, when you would be in the full spirit of prayer. Things more or less like this "I speak as a child." Let your imagination sweep up through the whole visible heavens, up to the heaven of heavens. Let her sweep and soar on her shining wing up past sun, moon, and stars. Let her leave Orion and the Pleiades far behind her. And let her heart swell and beat as she says such things as these to herself: "He made all these things—*He,* whom I now seek. That is

His sun. My Father made them all. My Mediator made them all to the glory of His Father. And He is the heir of all things. Oh to be at peace with the Almighty! Oh never again for one moment to forget or disobey or displease Him! Oh to be an heir with Jesus Christ! Oh to be found among the sons and the daughters of God Almighty!"

At another time, as you kneel down, flash, in a moment— I still speak as a child—the eyes of your heart back to Adam in his garden and with the image of God still in all its glory on him, and to Abraham over Sodom, and to Moses in the cleft of the rock, and to David in the night watches, and to Jesus Christ all night on the mountain top—and your time will not be lost. For, by such a flash of your imagination, at such a moment, the spirit of grace and supplication will be put in complete possession of your whole soul. Never open your eyes any morning without, that moment, seeing God and saying, "I laid me down and slept; I awaked; for the Lord sustained me." And never lie down without saying, "I will lay me down in both peace and sleep, for Thou, Lord, only makest me to dwell in safety." Never set out on a journey till you have said to God and to your own soul, "The Lord shall preserve thy going out and thy coming in from this time forth, and even for evermore." And never so much as say grace at table, however short the time you have to say it in, without seeing Him. In the twinkling of an eye be for one moment, if no more, with Him who spreads your table and makes your cup to run over. In short, be sure to get a true sight and a true hold of God, in some way or other, before you begin either prayer or praise. There is nothing in this world so difficult. The time it takes, sometimes, and the toil, and the devices, and the instrumentalities—you would not believe, because no word in all the Bible better describes us when we are at prayer, and at praise, and at table than this: "Without God"; and this: "Their hearts are far from me." Be sure, then—with all the help that heaven and earth, that God and man can give you—be sure you get your eyes and your hands on God in your prayer. You may begin and end your prayer without that, if you are in a hurry; and if you have no time or taste to give to Him who will be honored, and waited on, and well pleased with you. But, if so, you need not begin. It is not prayer at all. In an audience with an earthly sovereign you would not grudge or count up the time and the pains and the schooling beforehand. You would not begin to speak to him while yet you were in the street, or on the stair, or out among the common crowd. You would keep your cause in your heart till you were in his presence, and then, when you saw him sitting on his throne high up above you, you would fall down before him, and would fill your mouth with arguments.

Never say any of your idle words to Almighty God. Say your idle words to your equals. Say them to your sovereigns. But never, as you shall answer for it, never, all your days, to God. Set the Lord always before you. Direct your prayer to Him, and look up. Better be somewhat too bold and somewhat unseemly than altogether to neglect and forget Almighty God. Better say that so bold saying, "I will not let thee go," than pray with such laziness and sleepiness and stupidity as we now pray. Look for God, and look at God, till you can honestly say to Him, with Dr. Newman, a great genius and a great saint, that there are now, to you, two, and two only, supreme and luminously self-evident beings in the whole universe, yourself and your Creator. And when once you begin to pray in that way, you will know it. Every prayer of yours like that will ever after leave its lasting mark on you. You will not long remain the same man. Praying, with the imagination all awake and all employed—such praying will soon drink up your whole soul into itself. You will then "pray always." It will be to you by far the noblest and the most blessed of all your employments in this

present world. You will pray "without ceasing." We shall
have to drag you out of your closet by main force. You will
then be prayerful "over much." "Whether in the body I cannot tell; or whether out of the body, I cannot tell: God knoweth." Such will you all become when you accustom your
inward eyes to see and to brood continually on the power,
and on the greatness, and on the goodness, and on the grace,
and on the glory of God.

Yes, but all the time, what about this? you will ask—
what about this—that "no man hath seen God at any
time"? Well, that is true, and well remembered, and oppor-
tunely and appropriately brought forward. Whatever else
is true or false, *that* is true. That, all the time, abides the
deepest and the surest of truths. And thus it was that the In-
visible Father sent His Son to take our "opaque and pal-
pable" flesh and in it to reveal the Father. "And the Word
was made flesh, and dwelt among us, and we beheld his
glory." And it is this being "made flesh" of the Son of God
that has enabled us to see God. It is the birth and the whole
life, and the words, and the works, and the death, and the
resurrection, and the ascension, and the revelation from
heaven again of Jesus Christ—it is all this that has forever
opened up such new and boundless worlds which the Christian imagination may visit, and in which she may expatiate
and regale herself continually.

The absolute and pure Godhead is utterly and absolutely
out of all reach, even of the highest flights of the imagination of man. The pure and unincarnated Godhead dwells in
light which no man's imagination has ever seen even afar
off, or ever can see. But, then, hear this: "He that hath seen
me hath seen the Father." Well, if that is true, come
now! Awake up, O my baffled and beaten-back imagination!
Awake, and look at last on thy God! Awake, and feast
thyself for ever on thy God! Bathe, and sun, and satiate thyself to all eternity in the sweetness and in the beauty and

in the light and in the glory of thy God! There is nothing, in earth or in heaven, to our imagination now, like the *Word made flesh*. We cannot waste any more, not even so much as one beat of her wing or one glance of her eye, or one heave of her heart on any one, in heaven or earth, but the *Word made flesh*. "Whom have I in heaven but thee? And there is none upon earth that I desire beside thee."

There is a cold and heartless proverb among men to this effect: "Out of sight, out of mind." And this cold and heartless proverb would be wholly true—even of believing men —if it were not for the divine offices and the splendid services of the Christian imagination. But the truly Christian imagination never lets Jesus Christ out of her sight. And she keeps Him in her sight and ever before her inward eyes in this way. You open your New Testament—which is imagination's peculiar and most delightful field—you open that Book of books, say, at the beginning of the Sermon on the Mount. And, by your imagination, that moment you are one of Christ's disciples on the spot, and are at His feet. And during all that sermon you never once lift your eyes off the Great Preacher. You hear nothing else, and you see nothing else, till He shuts the Book and says, "Great was the fall of the house," and so ends His sermon. All through His sermon you have seen the working of His face. In every word of His sermon you have felt the beating of His heart. Your eye has met His eye, again and again, till you are in chains of grace and truth to Him ever after. And then, no sooner has He risen up and come down the hill than a leper, who dared not go up the hill, falls down at His feet, and says, "Lord, if thou wilt, thou canst make me clean!" And all your days, ever since that sermon, you are that leper. All that day you have been more and more like that leper, till now, as that day closes, you are like him nigh unto death. You worship Christ like the leper. He is beside you. He stands over you. You feel, as never before, the leprosy of sin. It fills full your polluted heart. The diseased flesh of that poor leper is the flesh of a little child compared with you and with your heart, till, in a more than leper-like loathing at yourself, and a more than leper-like despair of yourself, you bury your face before His feet and cry to Him: "But, Lord, if thou only wilt, thou canst make me clean!"

And so on, as often as, with your imagination anointed with holy oil, you again open your New Testament. At one time you are the publican; at another time you are the prodigal, at another time you are Lazarus in his grave, beside whose dead body it was not safe or fit for a living man to come; at another time you are Mary Magdalene, another time you are Judas with the money of the chief priest in his hand, and afterwards with his halter round his neck, till your whole New Testament is all over autobiographic of you, and till you can say to Matthew and Mark and Luke, and to John himself: Now I believe; and not for your sayings so much; for I have seen Him *myself,* and have *myself* been healed of Him, and *know* that this is indeed the Christ of God, and the Saviour of the world. Never, then, I implore you—I demand of you—never, all the days and nights that are left to you, never open your New Testament till you have offered this prayer to God the Holy Ghost: *"Open Thou mine eyes!"* And then, as you read, stop and ponder, stop and open your eyes, stop and imagine, stop till you actually *see* Jesus Christ in the same room with you. "Lo, I am with you alway." Ask Him, if He hides Himself from you, ask Him aloud, yes, aloud, whether these are, indeed, His words to you, or no. Expect Him. Rise up, and open to Him. Salute Him. Put down your book. Put down your light, and then say such things as these: "Jesus Christ! Son of David! Son of Mary! Carpenter's Son! Son of God! Saviour of sinners, of whom I am chief!" Speak it out. Do not be afraid that both men and devils hear thee speaking to thy Saviour. What about them all when thou art alone with the Son of God? And, besides, all men are asleep. "Art thou, in very truth, here, O Christ? Dost *Thou see me?* Dost *Thou* hear *me?* Yes! Thou art *here!* I am *sure* of it. I *feel* it. O blessed One! O Son of the Highest! I am not worthy that Thou shouldest come under my roof. But Thou art here! *Here,* of all the houses in the whole city! And here with *me,* O my Saviour, *with me* of all men in the whole city!" Fall at His feet, kiss His feet. Kiss His feet till thy lips come on an iron nail in them, and, after that, thou wilt know, of a truth, who He is that is with thee in the night watches!

But your absolutely highest, and absolutely best, and absolutely boldest use of your imagination has yet to be told, if you are able to bear it, and are willing to receive it. It is a very high and a very fruitful employment of your imagination to go back and to put yourself by means of it into the place of Adam, of Abraham, of Moses, of Job, and of Peter, of Judas, and of the Magdalene, and of the thief on the cross. But, to put out this magnificent talent to its very best usury, you must take the highest boldness in all the world, and put yourself in the place of *Christ Himself.* Put yourself and all that is within you into the hand of the Holy Ghost, and He will help you, most willingly and most successfully to imagine yourself to be Jesus Christ. Imagine yourself, then, to be in Nazareth, where He was brought up. Imagine yourself—and show to your son and your Sunday-school scholar the way to imagine himself—sitting beside Joseph and Mary every Sabbath day in that little synagogue. Imagine yourself to be the carpenter's son, as He was. Imagine yourself at Jordan at John's great awakening of the dry bones, and then at John's baptism. Imagine yourself fighting the devil in the wilderness with nothing but fasting and praying and the Word of God for weapons. Imagine yourself without where to lay your head. Imagine all your disciples turning against you and forsaking you. Imagine the upper room, and the garden, and the arrest and the Cross, and the darkness, and "My God, my God, why hast thou forsaken me?" Did you ever imagine yourself to be crucified? Paul did. And the imagination made him the matchless apostle of the Cross that he was. And then imagine yourself Christ risen, and in glory, and looking down on *your* heart, and on *your* life, and on *your* closet, and on *your* bed. Imagine Him seeing *you*—your mind, your heart, your inspiration, your motives, your intentions, your thoughts— all you think, and all you say, and all you do. And then I challenge you to imagine what He must be thinking and feeling, and making up His mind today as to what He is to say and to do to you, and when! What would you say about yourself if you were in His place, if you had died on the tree for such sins as yours, and then saw yourself what, all this time, you are, having no wish and no intention ever to be otherwise? I think you would throw down your office. I feel sure you would wash your hands of yourself. You would say, "Let him alone!" You would say, "Cut it down! Why cumbereth it the ground?" I will tell you literally and exactly what you would say. From God's Word I will tell you what any honest and earnest and wearied and insulted man would say, and what may this moment, for anything you know, be said over you from the great white throne of God: "Because I have called, and ye refused; I have stretched out my hand, and no man regarded. . . . I will laugh at your calamity; I will mock when your fear cometh; when your fear cometh as desolation, and your destruction cometh as a whirlwind. . . . For that they hated knowledge, and did not choose the fear of the Lord."

Imagine the Lamb in His wrath saying *that!* And imagine yourself dying, and not knowing at threescore and ten how to pray! Imagine yourself at the river, and no one there to meet you, no one to say to you, "I will be with thee"! Imagine the Judge in His hot anger saying it, and shutting to the door—"I never knew you"! And then imagine with all your might of imagination—imagine that, by an unparalleled act of God's grace, you are sent back again to this world, just for one more year, just for one more week, just for one more Sabbath day or Sabbath night! O prayer-neglecting sinner! O equally prayer-neglecting child of God! One more Sabbath day of the mercy seat, and the Mediator at God's right hand, and the Blood of Christ that speaketh peace!

"I have heard of thee by the hearing of the ear: but now, mine eye seeth thee. Wherefore I abhor myself, and repent in dust and ashes."

A Great Gospel Text

To him that worketh not, but believeth on him that justifieth the ungodly, His faith is counted for righteousness.

ROMANS 4: 5.

EVERY GREAT science, every great art, every great doctrine and discipline, has its own special terminology, its own technical terms, as we call them. Every new discovery, every new invention, every new doctrine, demands a new name to describe it, to contain it, and to convey it. Now, though it is quite true that this word "work" is one of our most familiar words, at the same time, when the Apostle takes that word up into his great evangelical vocabulary, he straightway fills that familiar word of ours full with all the fullness of his own inward and spiritual meaning. He fills it full with such new and such deep meanings that it takes us all our days to get this one word of his well into our so inexperienced and so unspiritual minds.

To work, in the ordinary and everyday sense of that word, is just to do this and that with our hands. It is to dig, and dress, and keep a garden. It is to plow, and sow, and reap. It is to found, and build, and furnish a house. As the fourth commandment has it, Six days shalt thou labor, and do all thy work. But there is a whole world of work that is not comprehended in the fourth commandment. Master, said one in the Gospel, which is the great commandment of the law? Jesus said to him, Thou shalt love the Lord thy God with all thy heart, and with all thy strength, and with all thy mind, and thy neighbor as thyself. Now, that is the commandment, and that is the work, which the Apostle is continually treating of, and not the six days' work of the fourth commandment. The grand commandment of love embraces not only all that we do both Sabbath day and week day, but, much more, all that we think both Sabbath day and week day, and all that we feel, and all that we desire, and all that we long after. To work, in the Apostle's employment of the word, is every beat of our heart, and every tone of our voice, and every glance of our eye; it is every sigh of ours and every smile. All we are, and all we have, and all we do, must be wholly given up to God and our neighbor, just as God gives up Himself and our neighbor to us. For God is love, and love is the fulfilling of all God's holy law.

Now, that being so, is it not very startling that the Apostle should say here what he does say in our text? That he should say this to him that worketh not, that is, to say to him who loves neither God nor his neighbor aright, such and such great blessings are offered to him, and are indeed pressed on him? What does the Apostle mean? One thing is certain, he cannot mean what, at first sight, he seems to mean. He cannot mean that the man who does not endeavor with all his might to love and serve both God and his neighbor can ever stand accepted before God. No. But he has the mind of Christ and the message of God to us when he says authoritatively and conclusively: to him that worketh not, that is to say, to him who cannot work, to him who, as God is his witness, would work if only he were able; to him who agonizes day and night to do this work of works, and who has forever given up agonizing after anything else; to him who sets God and his neighbor before him in everything, but finds that the things he fain would do, both to God and his neighbor, he cannot attain, even with all his sweat, and with all his tears, and with all his prayers. He works his fingers to the bone, he bows his back to the burden, but with it all, and after it all, at the end of every day he lays down his day's work toward God and his neighbor, not only not done, but much further from being done than it was when he took it up. Oh wretched man that he is, who shall deliver him from the body of this death? For we know that whatsoever the law saith, it saith to them that are under the law, that every mouth may be stopped and all the world become guilty before God.

But what is this that is here preached from God to every man whose mouth is so stopped? What is this new thing, "believing," to which such great blessings are everywhere promised? Well, the very first step of all believing to everlasting life is to believe what is written in the New Testament concerning Jesus Christ. At the same time, I may believe every word that Matthew and Mark and Luke and John ever wrote about Jesus of Nazareth, just as I believe what Plutarch and Tacitus wrote about Julius Cæsar, and yet be no better. That is to say, I may believe my New Testament with what our divines are wont to call a historic faith. Nay, I might even have actually stood on Calvary, and might have seen with my own eyes Jesus Christ on the Cross, and yet not have gone down to my house justified. To be justified by faith I must go on to believe that God has set forth His Son to be a propitiation for sin, through faith in His blood, and I must place all my faith in His blood as if He had come and had died on the Cross for me alone. As Walter Marshall has it: "The former of these acts of believing doth not immediately unite us to Christ, because it termineth only on the gospel. Yet it is a saving act, so far as it goes, because it instructeth and inclineth and disposeth the soul to the latter act, whereby Christ Himself is immediately received into the heart. He that believeth the New Testament with hearty love and liking, as the most excellent truth, will certainly, with the like heartiness, believe on Christ for his salvation." And thus true saving faith, once rooted in any man's heart, will, under the hand of the Holy Ghost, grow up to the full assurance of faith as we see it in such great examples of full assurance as Abraham, the father of the faithful in the Old Testament, and Paul himself, the great preacher and pattern of faith in the New Testament.

But though Walter Marshall is preaching Paul's gospel when he makes the saving act of faith to terminate on Christ and in His blood, at the same time, in this text, as so often in other texts, the Apostle carries our faith up beyond even Christ, and beyond even His blood, and rests it ultimately and finally on God the Father. In the Apostle's soteriology our salvation takes its first rise in the love and the grace of the Father, and then both the Son and the Spirit perform each their proper part in carrying out the Father's will. And thus it is that in this great text Paul runs our faith up to God the Father Himself, and instructs us to make our approach to Him alone as the "justifier of the ungodly." But we are staggered at that name of God, as at so many other of His names. When we first hear this immortal doctrine, the justification of the ungodly, we will not have it. In the interests of truth and righteousness, and for the honor of God, we will not listen to it. That the ungodly should be justified, and the ungodly alone—far be it from us to believe such antinomian teaching! We can understand the godly being justified, or even the partly godly and the partly ungodly; but not the utterly ungodly. But so it is. In the gospel this is one of the many mysteries of godliness, that God justifieth the ungodly, and the ungodly alone, and that as ungodly, and always as ungodly. The more ungodly indeed any man is, the more fit and eligible he is for justification. It was the godliness of the Pharisee that was his ruin. And it was the utter absence of all godliness in the publican that made it possible to send him to his house justified. And so is it in this temple today also. Show me the man among you who feels himself to be the most ungodly man in the whole congregation. Show me the man who feels himself to be absolutely made of sin, like David and Paul, and I will show you the man who is the ripest of you all for his free and full justification, and who, if he will only add to his utter ungodliness the faith of the text, will go down to his house established in that peace of conscience which passes all understanding.

This doctrine of justification by faith is like one of the doctrines of the old manuscripts. The more difficult it is to receive any offered reading of an old manuscript, the more unlikely it is to be true; the harder the lection, the more the scholars trust it, and take it, and incorporate it. Now, nothing is offered to us in the whole region of salvation so hard to receive, and believe, and hold by, as just the doctrine of the text. The Jews would not have it; they stoned Paul because he preached it. The whole apostleship itself was up in arms against him because of it. They condemned it as an antinomian doctrine, and they denounced him who preached it. But it held the field, and it will more and more hold the field wherever it is preached in faith and prayer, and alongside a holy life, as Paul preached it, and as Luther, and Hooker, and Bunyan, and Marshall, and all the Puritans, and Chalmers and all his sons, preached it in Scotland. "I should be glad to know," wrote Luther to Spentein, an Augustinian monk, "what is the state of your soul. When you and I were living together we were both in the greatest of all errors: seeking to stand before God on the ground of our own works. I am still struggling against that fatal error, and have not even yet entirely triumphed over it. O my dear brother, learn to know Jesus Christ, and Him crucified. Beware of pretending to such purity as no longer to confess thyself the chief of sinners. If our labors, and obediences, and afflictions, could have given peace to the con-

science, why should Christ have died on the cross? You will
never find true peace till you find it and keep it in this:
that Christ takes all your sins upon Himself, and bestows
all His righteousness on you." And when the Reformation
had brought back the pulpit of England to the Epistle to
the Romans, and to the article of a standing or falling
Church——Richard Hooker preached thus in his immortal
sermon on Justification—I feel as if I could never repeat the
passage too often—"Christ hath merited righteousness for
as many as are found in Him. And in Him God findeth us
if we be believers. For by believing we are incorporated into
Christ.

Then, although in ourselves we be altogether in ourselves we be altogether sinful and unrighteous, yet even the
man who is in himself impious, full of iniquity, full of sin;
him being found in Christ through faith, and having his
sins in hatred through repentance—him God beholdeth
with a gracious eye, and accepteth him in Jesus Christ, as
perfectly righteous as if he had fulfilled all that is commanded in the holy law of God—shall I say accepteth him
as more perfectly righteous than if himself had fulfilled the
whole law? I must take heed what I say; but the Apostle
saith, 'God hath made him to be sin for us, who knew no
sin; that we might be made the righteousness of God in
him!' Let it be counted folly, or frenzy, or fury, or whatsoever; it is our wisdom and our comfort. We care for no
knowledge in the world but this: that man hath sinned and
God hath suffered: that God hath made Himself the sin of
men, and that men are made the righteousness of God."

The Blood of God

The church of God, which he hath purchased with his own blood.

ACTS 20: 28.

THERE IS a well-known device in first-class composition whereby a great author gives his readers a sudden stroke of surprise, which is the substitution of a different name for that of the person of whom he is writing. All our best literature is full of this ancient rhetorical device; Holy Scripture is full of it, and the text is a case in point. The readers of the Apostle would have expected him to say: The Church of God, which he hath purchased with the blood of his Son, or with the blood of Jesus Christ, or with the blood of the Lamb. But by this new and unique way in which the Apostle words this great scripture, he startles his readers into still more wonder and worship than if he had been content to employ one of those far more usual names of our Lord. In this very bold passage the Apostle sets the sin-atoning death of Jesus Christ before us with the veil of His flesh withdrawn, as it were, for a moment. In this almost too bold scripture, he sets before us the pure and immediate Godhead of our Lord made sin for us. And the immense impression that these almost too awful words, "the blood of God," make on our minds and our hearts as often as we return to them, is the Apostle's complete justification and rich reward for his almost too bold employment of them.

1. Now, in the first place, what an unspeakable evil sin

must be! We would not have been altogether ignorant of the awful evil of sin, even if it had not gone the length of the blood of God. We could not have shut our eyes to the way that sin has cursed and enslaved the soul of man. Death here, and hell hereafter, would surely have burned something of the diabolical evil of sin into the most sin-seared conscience and into the most stone-hardened heart. But all the sickbeds, and all the deathbeds, and all the lazar houses, and all the madhouses, and all the battlefields, and all the desolated homes, and all the broken hearts of men and women, from the fall of man to the day of judgment, would not have proclaimed to earth and heaven and hell the unspeakable malice and wickedness of sin. God's own blood, shed by sin, and shed for sin—that alone, in all the universe, is the full measure of the infinite evil of sin. "Whatever your thoughts about sin may be; whatever your experience and estimate of sin may be, that is my experience and estimate of sin," says Almighty God, pointing us to Gethsemane and to Calvary. God the Son made a curse, that and that alone is the true measure of sin; that and that alone has forever revealed the true evil of sin; and that and that alone has paid the uttermost farthing for our everlasting redemption and deliverance from sin. "Let it be counted folly, or frenzy, or fury, or whatsoever," says Hooker, in what is perhaps the greatest sermon in the English language, "it is our wisdom and our comfort. We care for no other knowledge in the world but this, that man hath sinned and God hath suffered: that God hath made Himself the sin of men, and that men are made the righteousness of God."

2. And then what a glorious seal has been set to the holiness of the law of God by His own blood. No wonder that the holy law of God was proclaimed to be magnified, and made honorable forever, when the very blood of the Lawgiver Himself was shed in order to vindicate and redress

the broken law. The throne of God had been founded in righteousness from everlasting. But after a full satisfaction for sin had been made with His own blood who had sat on that throne from everlasting, that glorious throne was forever established in righteousness as never before. How surpassingly illustrious has the holiness of the law of God shone out on all earth and heaven ever since that day when He whose law it was, shed His own blood in atonement to the holiness and the inviolability of that law!

And not His own blood at its last and completed outpouring only. But, along with that, take all the things of the same kind that led up to His bloodshedding on the tree, and all the things that entered into that last bloodshedding. Take all His holy obedience, and all His holy endurance of all kinds in His body, and in His soul, and in His spirit, from His circumcision to His crucifixion. For all that was paid by Him, first in tribute, and then in atonement, to His own holy law. And it was all paid for us. Is all our daily and hourly sin so much bold rebellion against the complete, and perfect, and most willing subjection and obedience in everything of God the Son? Are we by nature, and on every temptation to it, full of malice toward God and man? Look, over against that, at our Lord's love to God and man. Look at His unbounded goodness of heart and life. Is there bitter repining, and envying, and grudging in our hearts at the good of our neighbor? Then let us lift our eyes and look at the Son of God, how He made Himself of no reputation, and rejoiced at the prospect of His sharing His glory with us all forever. Hear Him, O jealous and grudging hearts! "I thank thee, O Father, that thou hast loved them as thou hast loved me." And so on through the whole of His life of suretyship obedience, and on to the end of His death of atonement, till His own holy law was satisfied and vindicated to its very utmost height and depth and length and breadth, even to its very innermost spirituality, in every thought and word and deed of God the Son as the son of man.

3. But the sinner's guilty conscience is sometimes, and in some men, far more difficult to satisfy and to silence than even the broken law of God. Long after the broken law of God has been magnified and made honorable, the sinner's evil conscience will still hold out against all that can be said or done to restore its lost peace, and to reestablish its lost confidence in the good will of God and man. There is a divinely delegated sovereignty in the human conscience, and there is a corresponding uncompromisingness and inappeasableness in the guilty conscience. Even after the offended sovereign is satisfied, the viceroy still holds out against the disloyalty and the treachery. The *crimen laesae majestatis,* the high misdemeanor done against the crown, is far more resented and avenged by the king's judges than even by the king himself. And sin is such an unpardonable misdemeanor against all law and all authority, and it so gashes the conscience and so horrifies the heart of the truly penitent sinner, that absolutely nothing has ever been discovered to heal and to quiet and to restore the conscience but the blood of Him who is God. There is no physician for the sinner's exasperated conscience, as Luther is always saying, but the Lord of the conscience Himself. And there is no balm that even He can bring to bear on a thoroughly bad conscience but His own blood. Your guilty conscience can have nothing better than the blood of your God. And if that does not cleanse, and quiet, and heal your guilty conscience, it must just rage on. Your conscience can be offered nothing on earth or in heaven beyond the blood of God.

4. One of the ways in which the blood of God comes to have such sovereign virtue in the sinner's conscience is this: when our consciences toward one another are wounded, and are full of remorse and fear, nothing will heal the wound and restore peace between man and man, nothing

but a great uprising of love between the alienated parties. But if a great enough uprising and outgoing of love takes place between them, then not only is the lost peace restored, but those who were once such enemies are henceforth far better friends than ever they were before. And the same noble law of reconciling love holds even more in the world of sin and salvation. The blood of God the Son is such a manifestation of divine love toward the sinner that nothing can resist it. No guilt, no remorse, no terror, no suspicion, can stand out against the love of God in the blood of His only begotten Son. It is not so much our Surety's payment of the uttermost farthing of our debt that heals our horrified consciences. It is not His atoning blood even that so pacifies, and so conquers, and gives such peace to, the guilty conscience. It is only the love of God as seen in the atonement that can do all that. And if there are still any of the dregs of remorse, and terror, and irreconcilability, and suspicion in your conscience toward God, it is not because His blood is not of volume and virtue enough to wash away all your sins, but it is because you do not open your heart wide enough and deep enough to receive His love. For there is no fear in love. But perfect love on God's part to you, awakening on your part a corresponding love to God, such perfect love on both sides casteth out all possible fear, so much so, that he that feareth is not made perfect in love.

My brethren, I can recommend this great scripture in every guilty conscience and corrupt heart. For, times and occasions without number, when every other scripture has threatened to fail myself, this scripture has been a rock and a refuge to me. The very awfulness of the word used has again and again silenced the almost as awful accusation of my conscience and the almost as awful despair of my heart. I know all that has been said against the above reading in this glorious passage; but once read by me I shall never let it go, though I have to hold it against all the world. The *Blood of God* has an inward, and an experimental, and an all-satisfying evidence to me, and I recommend it to you with all my heart.

The Strappado

All my bones are out of joint.
PSALM 22:14.

IN OLD and evil days there was a diabolical instrument of torture in Spain called the strappado. And that cruel instrument was worked in this wicked way: the poor victim was first hoisted up to a great height, by means of ropes and pulleys, and then he was suddenly dashed to the ground, till every bone in his body was torn out of joint and broken in pieces. And the name of the Spanish strappado has passed into the English language, because the old preachers of that day frequently employed the illustration of the strappado in their experimental sermons. As thus Goodwin: "Now, his lusts, both of body and mind, do strappado a sinner's expectations. That is to say: his sinful imaginations hoist up his expectations of pleasure to a great height; and then, suddenly, he is let fall. For, when the sinner comes to enjoy his high expectations, they always prove themselves to be such flat and empty things, that his soul, being completely cheated, says to itself, And is this all! Thus, always, do a sinner's high expectations strappado him, till his spirit is simply dashed to pieces within him."

So far as I know, the Spanish strappado was never imported into Scotland or England. But if we have not the scaffoldings and the pulleys, and the ropes of that inhuman instrument among us, we have plenty of those personal experiences which are so vividly and so forcibly illustrated by those scaffoldings and pulleys and ropes and broken bones. For we have plenty of high expectations followed by deep disappointments, plenty of great and towering ambitions followed by great depressions, plenty of high hopes followed by low despairs, plenty of seekings of great things for ourselves followed by small and heart-starving results, till it has been powerfully impressed on me that the Spanish strappado may have some important lessons to read to us in our own land and in our own day.

Well, to begin with, such are we, and such is this present life of ours, that lawful enough pursuits and lawful enough pleasures not seldom become our very worst strappados. As Goodwin says: "Pleasures that are quite lawful to us become altogether unlawful and unsatisfying when our affections and our imaginations are too frequently and too vehemently set upon them." There is no need for me to put a name on such pleasures: every man's own conscience will name them to him. The sweetest and the most allowable thing on earth has become an absolute strappado to some men. I will not name it, lest you be not able to bear it. But all readers of Luther will remember that he is very bold about it, and tells us his own strappadic experience of it.

Again, in a commercial country like ours, first the pursuit of wealth, and then the possession of wealth, strappado many men's souls. Many such men have lived to confess, and say that when they were children, they thought as children and understood as children. They thought, when they had attained to great wealth, how happy they would be. They thought that when once they had a great house full of vessels of gold and silver, with horses and carriages at their doors, and troops of friends around their table, then it would be heaven on earth with them. But when they became rich men, all those childish visions of perfect blessedness fled away. The Psalmist saw multitudes of such strappadoed men all around him in his day, and his lament over them was this: "Verily every man, at his best estate, is altogether vanity. Surely every man walketh in a vain show: surely they are disquieted in vain: he heapeth up riches, and knoweth not who shall gather them." And our Lord also has this warning word to all such men: "Thou fool, this night thy soul shall be required of thee: then whose shall those things be, which thou hast provided?" At the same time, there is no nobler pursuit on earth than the pursuit of riches if they are pursued in order that they may be spent on God and man, on the Church of Christ, and on His poor. The higher such men climb, the nearer heaven they rise, and they shall never know disappointment or defeat. All success to all such men as work with their hands, or with their heads, that they may have to give to him that needeth!

On another side of human life, what a strappado the pursuit of praise and fame is to many men among us. Take this true illustration. A friend of mine, a minister in England, became absolutely intoxicated with the ambition to write a great book on a great subject. When, after years of neglect of his pulpit and his pastorate in his devotion to his book, he was in Edinburgh and called on me, for hour after hour he poured out to me about his coming masterpiece. But when it came out, his book received only one little scurvy review in one obscure London newspaper. When I next saw my friend I scarcely knew him, so shrunk was he, both in body and in mind. He was like our text: he had had such a fall that all his bones were out of joint.

You will often see the same thing in preachers and public speakers. A member of Assembly, say, has labored for weeks at a great speech which is to make his reputation. But when he enters the advertised hall he finds it empty. And he suffers such a fall from his pride that moment that he can scarcely command his strength enough to finish the fourth part of what he had written with such labor and such expectation. The pulpit also is the sure strappado of the popularity-hunting preacher. Even if he is puffed up for a time, the hour soon comes for another to arise who wholly eclipses him, till he lies with broken bones at the foot of his forgotten and forsaken pulpit. The higher his ambition hoisted him up, the deeper and the more heart-breaking is his fall. Let these examples of strappado suffice. Every man whose eyes are open will see plenty of such examples all around him. And he is a happy man who is not such an example himself.

"God," says Goodwin, "had a whole book written about the strappado in Israel, and He employed King Solomon to be His penman in that pathetic book. No man was ever hoisted higher than King Solomon, and no man ever had a sadder fall. Just hear Solomon about himself in that matter. 'I said in my heart, Go to, now, I will prove thee with mirth, therefore enjoy pleasure. . . . I sought in mine heart to give myself unto wine. . . . I made me great works; I builded me houses; I planted me vineyards: . . . I got me servants and maidens, and had servants born in my house; also I had great possessions of great and small cattle above all that were in Jerusalem before me: I gathered me also silver and gold: . . . I gat me men singers and women singers, and the delights of the sons of men. . . . So I was great, and I increased more than all that were before me in Jerusalem. . . . And whatsoever mine eyes desired I kept not from them. I withheld not my heart from any joy.'" And so on—chapter after chapter.

Don't you envy Solomon? We all do. But Solomon's book is not yet finished. For, as we read on, we come to this: "Then I looked on all the works that my hands had wrought: and, behold, all was vanity and vexation of spirit, and there was no profit under the sun. Therefore I hated my life, because it was all vanity and vexation of spirit. He that loveth silver shall not be satisfied with silver, nor he that loveth abundance with increase: this also is vanity.

The sleep of a labouring man is sweet, whether he eat little or much; but the abundance of the rich man will not suffer him to sleep. Vanity of vanities, saith the preacher, all is vanity." The word "strappado" is not found in all the Hebrew Bible; but the thing was never better experienced and described than in the words of the Preacher, the son of David, King in Jerusalem. Just read his bitter book for yourselves and see how full of lessons it is to you all, be you king or subject, laboring man or master, rich or poor, young or old.

There is not much that can properly be called Gospel in Solomon's autobiography. At the same time the Preacher was not left wholly without hope for himself, and for men like himself. And what light there is in his dark book is all the brighter because of its so black background. For Solomon's own sake we seize eagerly on such utterances of his broken heart as these: "I came to see," he says, "that wisdom excelleth folly, as light excelleth darkness." And again: "God hath made everything beautiful in its season: and it is God's will that every man should enjoy the good of his labour: and a man's labour, and his good from it, are the gifts of God to him." Again: "Better is an handful with quietness to enjoy it, than both hands full, with travail and vexation of spirit." Again: "Better is a poor man, if he is a wise man, than an old and foolish king, who will not be admonished." And this comes in about public worship, to which Solomon betook himself when he learned the vanity of life without religion: "Keep thy foot when thou goest to the house of God, and be more ready to hear than to give the sacrifice of fools. Be not rash with thy mouth, and let not thine heart be hasty to utter anything before God: for God is in heaven, and thou upon earth: therefore let thy words be few." Also: "When thou vowest a vow to God, defer not to pay it: pay that which thou hast vowed."

And, with all his disappointments in life, Solomon was

not so embittered as you would expect to see him. "Behold it is good and comely for a man to eat and to drink, and to enjoy the good of all his labour. Every man also, to whom God hath given riches and wealth, let him rejoice and enjoy his riches: for they are the gift of God." And again that beautiful passage: "Go thy way, eat thy bread with joy, and drink thy wine with a merry heart. Let thy garments be always white: and let thy head lack no ointment. Live joyfully with the wife thou lovest. And whatsoever thy hand findeth to do, do it with all thy might." Again: "A good name is better than riches." Again: "In the day of prosperity be joyful: but in the day of adversity consider." Again: "Cast thy bread upon the waters: for thou shalt find it after many days. In the morning sow thy seed, and in the evening withhold not thine hand." And then, that noble passage so nobly worded: "Remember now thy Creator in the days of thy youth, while the evil days come not, nor the years draw nigh, when thou shalt say, I have no pleasure in them: while the sun, or the light, or the moon, or the stars, be not darkened, nor the clouds return after the rain: or ever the silver cord be loosed, or the golden bowl be broken, or the pitcher be broken at the fountain: or the wheel broken at the cistern. Then shall the dust return to the earth as it was: and the spirit shall return unto God who gave it. The preacher sought to find out acceptable words; and that which was written was upright, even words of truth. Let us hear the conclusion of the whole matter: Fear God, and keep his commandments: for this is the whole duty of man." Happy he who has learned such wisdom as that out of all his liftings up and castings down!

The Ransom

To give his life a ransom for many.
MATTHEW 20: 28.

Let us draw near this morning and join ourselves to our Lord when He is on His way up to the Passover for the last time. And let us abide near Him this morning till we see the end. And when we see the end, let us all say for ourselves what Paul said for himself: "He loved me and gave himself for me."

1. No sooner had our Lord entered Jerusalem in the beginning of that week than, in His own words, He began "to give his life a ransom." So long as His time had not yet come, our Lord took great care of His life. His was the most precious life on the face of the earth, and He took correspondingly care of it. But now that the work of His life was finished, He began at once to give His life away. All the beginning and middle of that Passover week our Lord was preaching all the daytime in the Temple—and then at night He went out and abode in the mount that is called the Mount of Olives. All that week our Lord preached all day and prayed all night. Now, there is nothing so exhausting as preaching unless it is praying, such preaching, that is, and such praying as our Lord's preaching and praying were all that Passover week. Paul, in one place, speaks about preaching the "terror of the Lord." And that terrible word best describes our Lord's last sermons in Jerusalem. It is remarkable—and there must be a good reason for it—that the only sermons of our Lord that we have anything like

a full report of are His first sermon and His last—His Sermon on the Mount and His three days of farewell sermons in the Temple. That preacher was simply throwing his life away who delivered the discourses that Matthew has preserved in the end of his Gospel. He was walking straight into the jaws of death who stood up in the Temple—especially when there was not standing room in its passover-porches—and spoke the parable of "The Wicked Husbandman," and the parable of "The Marriage Feast," and the parable of "The Ten Virgins," and the parable of "The Last Judgment." And then, to make it impossible that His meaning could be missed, He hurled out such bolts of judgment as these: "Woe unto you, scribes and Pharisees, hypocrites! Woe! Woe! Woe!" For three whole days the terrible Preacher was permitted to anticipate the Last Day, and no man laid hands on Him. And then, all night in the Mount of Olives, our Lord, all that week, was simply squandering away what remained of His life. Unless, indeed, He was in all that ransoming the lost lives of those preachers who tune their pulpits and who, once they are home from their day's work and have well dined, will not after venture out again, either to preach or to pray. The Son of man gave His life for many ministers, in the Temple and in the garden, as well as on the tree.

2. The calmness of mind and the careful deliberation with which our Lord goes about the Last Supper is very affecting and very impressive. The quiet and orderly way in which He gives his instructions about the Supper, the serene and stately way in which He performs His whole part in the Upper Room, the watchful solicitude He shows about the behavior of the disciples, both to Himself and to one another, while all the time His own terrible death was just at the door—it melts our hearts to see it all. He dwells on the Supper. He lingers over the Supper. He lengthens it out. He takes it up, part after part. He looks

back at Moses in Egypt. He looks forward to the marriage supper of the Lamb. He legislates for the future of His ransomed Church and people. He takes the paschal lamb out of the Supper, and He puts Himself in its place. "Take, eat, this is my body broken for you. This is my blood of the New Testament," said the Lamb of God, "shed for many, for the remission of sins: drink ye all of it. And do this till I come." What a heart-melting sight! What nobleness! What peace! What beauty of holiness! What boundless love!

3. "Then cometh Jesus with them to a place called Gethsemane, and saith to the disciples, Sit ye there, while I go and pray yonder." Our Lord is in no mood for mockery, but our hearts read their own bitterness into His departing words. He seeks out a seat for the disciples. He seeks out the best, the softest, and the most sheltered seat in the garden. He points them to the place, and He bids them sit down in it. He tells them to keep near one another, and to keep one another company. And before He has got to His place "yonder," they are all fast asleep! *He* has not slept for a week. Night after night He has spent in the same spot, till even Judas "knew the place." More than the city watchmen for the morning, He had waited for God in that garden all that week, and He still waits. "Out of the depths have I cried to thee, O Lord. Out of the belly of hell, O Lord. Then I said, I am cast out of thy sight. The waters compassed me about even to the soul: the weeds were wrapped about my head." And being in an agony, He prayed more earnestly, and His sweat was as it were great drops of blood falling to the ground. It was the wages of sin. It was the Lord laying on Himself the iniquities of us all. It was—every ransomed soul knows what it was! "Yes, it was *my* cup," says every ransomed soul. "I mingled it, I filled it, I have sometimes just tasted it. No wonder He loathed it. No wonder He put it away. No wonder He sweat blood as He drank it. For that cup was *sin*. It was the wages

of my sin. It was full of the red wine of the wrath of God against me." And when He rose off His face and left the trampled-down and blood-soaked wine-press, He found the disciples still sleeping. And again our hearts mock at us as He says, "Sleep on now, and take your rest."

4. Were you ever false as hell to your best friend? Did you ever take your unsuspecting friend by the hand and say, "Welcome," or "Farewell"? Was there ever a sweet smile on your face while there was a dagger under your cloak? Did envy, or ambition, or revenge, or some such undiluted and downright devil ever enter your heart—till you almost went out and hanged yourself with horror at yourself? Then thou art the man that Jesus Christ ransomed from the halter and from hell when He submitted His cheek to the kiss of the traitor. It is because Jesus Christ has you and so many like you among His disciples that He took so meekly the diabolical embrace of the son of perdition. "It was not an enemy that reproached me: then I could have borne it: neither was it he that hated me that did magnify himself against me: then would I have hid myself from him. But it was thou, a man, mine equal, my guide and mine acquaintance. We took sweet counsel together, and walked into the house of God in company. Yea, mine own familiar friend, in whom I trusted, which did eat of my bread, hath lifted up his heel against me." "For we ourselves also were sometimes living . . . in malice and envy, hateful, and hating one another. But after that the kindness and love of God our Saviour toward man appeared, not by works of righteousness which we have done, but according to his mercy he saved us, by the washing of regeneration, and renewing of the Holy Ghost; which he shed on us abundantly through Jesus Christ our Saviour; that being justified by his grace, we should be made heirs according to the hope of eternal life."

5. "Then the band, and the captain and the officers of the

Jews, took Jesus and bound him." It is a very bitter moment
to a prisoner when the officers of justice are binding him.
I have often thought that the pinioning before execution
must be almost more dreadful than the very drop itself.
And our Lord felt most acutely the shame and the disgrace
of the prison shackles. For once He broke silence and spoke
out and remonstrated. "Be ye come out as against a thief?"
He turned on the officers. He had no intention of trying to
escape. He had come out to the garden to give Himself up.
He had said just the moment before, "I am he: take me;
and let these go their way." But the officers were under the
instructions of Judas. Their superiors in the city had told
them that they were to look to Judas for all their orders that
night. And Judas had said to the officers: "Whomsoever I
shall kiss, that same is he: take him and lead him away
safely: that same is he, hold him fast." And they obeyed
Judas; they held Him as fast and as safe as their best prison
cords could hold Him. O officers, officers! Judas must surely
know; but it is impossible that you can know why it is that
your prisoner walks with you so willingly. Did any of you
Roman officers ever hear of "cords of love"? Well, it is in
the cords of everlasting love that you keep your man so
safely tonight. O officers, officers! if only you knew who
that is you are leading in cords into the city! O Judas,
Judas! What are thy thoughts? O! Better never to have
been born!

6. "And all his disciples forsook him and fled. But Peter
followed him afar off, unto the high priest's palace, and
went in and sat with the servants to see the end." Did you
ever deny a friend? Did you ever sit still and hear a friend
of yours slandered, witnessed against by hired witnesses,
and condemned? Did you ever sit and warm yourself at
some man's fire, or, more likely, at some man's wine; and
for fear, for cowardice, or for the sake of the company and
the good cheer did you nod and smile and wink away your

absent brother's good name? Look, redeemed dastard, look at thy dreadful ransom! Look at Jesus Christ in the hard hands, and under the hired tongues of His assassins—and Peter, His sworn friend, washing his hands of all knowledge of the friendless Prisoner! Look, O dog in the shape of a man! All their sham charges, all their lying witnesses, all their judicial insults and brutalities are clean forgotten by Peter's Master! He does not hear what they are saying, and He does not care. A loud voice out in the porch has stabbed our Lord's heart to death. "I know not the man!" And the cock crew. And the Lord turned and looked upon Peter. And Peter went out and wept bitterly. And as the fine legend has it, Peter never heard a cock crow, day or night, all his days, that he did not remember the passover-porch of Caiaphas the High Priest that year in Jerusalem!

7. You have heard sometimes about hell being let loose. Yes, but hear this. Come to Caiaphas' palace on the passover night, and look at this. "Then did they spit in his face, and buffeted him: they blindfolded him and then they smote him with the palms of their hands, saying, Prophesy to us, thou Christ, who is it that smote thee. And they stripped him and put on him a scarlet robe. And when they had platted a crown of thorns"—I wonder in what sluggard's garden it grew—"they put it upon his head, and a reed in his right hand: and they bowed the knee before him, and mocked him, saying, Hail, King of the Jews! And they spit upon him, and took the reed out of his hand, and smote him on the head. Then Pilate took Jesus and scourged him. After which they brought Jesus forth wearing the crown of thorns and the purple robe. And when the chief priests saw Jesus, they cried out, Crucify him, crucify him! Then Pilate delivered him to them to be crucified." My brethren, these are dreadful, most dreadful, things. And all the time, God Almighty, the God and Father of Jesus Christ, restrained Himself; He held Himself

in, and sat as still as a stone, seeing and hearing all that. The arrest, the trial, the buffeting, the spitting, the jesting and the jeering, the bloody scourging, the crown of thorns, the reed, and the purple robe. Why? In the name of amazement, why did the Judge of all the earth sit still and see all that said and done? Do you know what made Him sit still? Did you ever think about it? And would you like to be told how it could be? God Almighty, my brethren, not only sat still, but He ordained it all; and His Son *endured* it all— *in order to take away sin,* to take away the very existence of sin forever. You will find the explanation of that terrible night's work, and of the still more terrible morning just about to dawn—you will find the explanation, the justification, and the complete key to it all *in your own heart.*

Did you ever see yourself to be such a despicable creature that you wondered why all men did not spit on you? Did you ever wonder that, not friendship and family life only, but very human society itself, did not dissolve and fall in pieces, such are the meanness, the despicableness, the duplicity, the selfishness, the cruelty, and the diabolical wickedness of the human heart—but, above all human hearts, of yours? You will understand the spitting scene that night when God lets you see your own heart. There was no surplus shame, there was no scorn too much; the contumely was not one iota overdone that night. There was no unnecessary disgrace poured on Christ that night. They are in every congregation, at every Communion table, and they are the salt and the ornament of it who say as they sit down at the table: He hid not His face from shame and from spitting for me! He loved me in my sin and my shame, and He gave Himself for me!

8. If all that will not melt your heart of stone, try the next thing that Pilate and his devils did. For Pilate scourged Him. I will leave the scourging to yourselves to picture, and to ask, What is scourging? Who was it that was that morn-

ing scourged? And why was He scourged, being innocent? And the crown of thorns, and all the awful scene to the end! O that mine head were waters and mine eyes a fountain of tears!

9. But come out to Calvary at nine o'clock that morning if you would be absolutely glutted with sorrow and with love. All the shame, all the scorn, all the horror, all the agony due to our sin, and undertaken by our Surety—it all met on the Cross. The Cross was the vilest, the cruellest, the most disgraceful, the most diabolical instrument of execution that ever hell had invented and set up on earth. Stand back and let the chiefest sinner in this house come forward. Give him the best place. Whoever sees the crucifixion, let *him* see it. Look, sinner, and see. They lay the Cross on the ground. They then take the cords off our Lord's pinioned arms, and the painted board off His breast. They then lay Him down on His back on the Cross; they stretch out His arms along the arms of the Cross. They then open out His hands; and with a hammer they drive a great nail of iron through His right hand, with the blood spurting up in their faces, and another through His left hand, and another through His feet, placed the one above the other to save the nails. Five or six strong soldiers then lift up the Cross with its trembling, bleeding Burden, and sink it down with a dash into the stone socket, set in the earth, till all His bones are out of joint. And "they know not what they do," is all He says. No, *they* know not, but the chief of sinners now looking on, he knows. Paul knew. "He loved me," said Paul, "and gave himself for me." Cowper knew:

> There is a fountain filled with blood
>   Drawn from Immanuel's veins;
> And sinners, plunged beneath that flood,
>   Lose all their guilty stains.

We often pray that God would "make the bed" of His dying saints, and He does it. But that was the deathbed God made for His dying Son!

But all that, after all, was but the outer porch of death to our Lord. Gethsemane and Caiaphas and Pilate and Herod's palace were but the outer court of the temple. The Cross was the altar, and the sacrifice began to be fully offered only about the sixth hour, when there was darkness over all the earth till the ninth hour. It passeth all understanding, and all the power of tongue and pen, what the Son of God suffered in body and in soul during those three dark and silent hours. Only at the ninth hour Jesus cried with a loud voice, "My God, my God, why hast thou forsaken me?" And some time after, "It is finished," when He bowed His head and gave up the ghost.

> 'Tis finished—was His latest voice:
>   These sacred accents o'er,
> He bowed His head, gave up the ghost,
>   And suffered pain no more.

> 'Tis finished: The Messiah dies
>   For sins, but not His own:
> The great redemption is complete
>   And Satan's power o'erthrown.

"So, after he had taken his garments and was set down again, he said unto them, Know ye what I have done to you?"

Yea, Lord. Thou hast given Thy life a ransom for many. Thou hast loved me and given Thyself for me!

> I am not worthy, holy Lord,
>   That Thou shouldst come to me;
> Speak but the word; one gracious word
>   Can set the sinner free.

I am not worthy; cold and bare
  The lodging of my soul;
How canst Thou deign to enter there?
  Speak, Lord, and make me whole.

I am not worthy; yet, my God,
  How can I say Thee nay,
Thee, who didst give Thy flesh and blood
  My ransom price to pay?

O come, in this sweet morning hour
  Feed me with food Divine,
And fill with all Thy love and power
  This worthless heart of mine.

In the Swelling of Jordan

How wilt thou do in the swelling of Jordan?
JEREMIAH 12:5.

Both in its disputed rise, and in its zigzag course, and then in its inscrutable fall, the Jordan is the most wonderful and, indeed, in some respects, the most mysterious river on the face of the earth. Rising among the obscure rocks and tangled forests of the Lebanon, the Jordan rushes down through a deep and a tortuous gorge, that seldom has seen a bridge, and that only here and there has admitted a ford for the foot of man or beast. Walled in by high and over-hanging rocks, the Jordan runs its crooked and angry course for some two hundred miles, till it loses itself in the Salt Sea, the Dead Sea of Sodom and Gomorrah. It was the absolutely miraculous passage of the Jordan by Joshua and the priests and the people of Israel that gave the river such a place of wonder and of praise in the prophets and psalmists of Israel. And as time went on, the passage of the Jordan became a proverb and a prophecy of the passing of the immortal soul out of this life of bitter bondage and of long and sore pilgrimage into the Promised Land, the Promised Land of our Heavenly Father's House. And so the prophet's solemnizing challenge, *"How wilt thou do in the swelling of Jordan?"* has come powerfully home to every man who has an evil conscience, and who has it before him to die and to go to judgment.

Well, then, before we come to *ourselves,* let us take a few moments to look at how some of our forerunners did when *they* came to the swelling of *their* "Jordan." And, first, let us look at our blessed Lord Himself, when He was approaching the dark river of death. For though He had no sin of His own to burden His conscience and to darken His heart, yet, at the same time, He was made such a surety and such a substitute for sinners that the swelling of His Jordan became an agony, and, indeed, a terror to Him, so much so that even the pen of inspiration trembles to describe His dying experiences. Listen, then, with all the holy fear you can command, to what is tremblingly written concerning even the "Jordan" of our sinless Lord. "Now is my soul troubled; and what shall I say? Father, save me from this hour." "Then took he with Him Peter and the two sons of Zebedee, and began to be sorrowful and very heavy. Then saith he unto them, My soul is exceeding sorrowful, even unto death: tarry ye here, and watch with me. And he went a little farther, and fell on his face, and prayed, saying, O my Father, if it be possible, let this cup pass from me: nevertheless not as I will, but as thou wilt." As Mark has it, "He began to be sore amazed, and to be very heavy." And as Luke has it, "Being in an agony he prayed more earnestly: and his sweat was as it were great drops of blood falling to the ground. . . . And on the morrow, when it was about the sixth hour, there was a great darkness over all the land until the ninth hour. And the sun was darkened, and the veil of the temple was rent in the midst. And, when he had received the vinegar, Jesus cried with a loud voice and said, Father, into thy hands I commend my spirit: and having said this, he gave up the ghost." Now that, my brethren, was somewhat of how our Lord did in the swelling of *His* Jordan.

"And one of the malefactors which were crucified beside him railed on him, and said, If thou be Christ, save thyself and us. But the other answering rebuked him, saying, Dost not thou fear God, seeing thou art in the same condemnation? And we indeed justly; for we receive the due reward of our deeds: but this man hath done nothing amiss. And he said unto Jesus, Lord, remember me when thou comest into thy kingdom. And Jesus said to him, Verily I say unto thee, Today shalt thou be with me in paradise." And *that* was how the penitent thief did in the swelling of *his* Jordan.

And *this* is how Stephen, the martyr deacon, did. After he had spoken his great speech, his enemies were cut to the heart, and they rose on him with one accord, and cast him out of the city, and stoned him to death; and he died calling on God, and saying, "Lord Jesus, receive my spirit, and lay not this sin to their charge." And they laid down their clothes at a young man's feet, whose name was Saul. And thirty years after that, Saul, by that time called Paul, descended into *his* Jordan with these words: "I thank Christ Jesus our Lord for putting me into the ministry; me who was before a blasphemer and a persecutor: but I obtained mercy, that in me Jesus Christ might show forth all long-suffering for a pattern to them which should hereafter believe on him to life everlasting. . . . And now I am ready to be offered, and the time of my departure is at hand. . . . Henceforth there is laid up for me a crown of righteousness, which the Lord, the righteous judge, shall give me at that day: and not to me only, but unto all them also that love his appearing."

When Augustine saw that the swelling of *his* Jordan was fast approaching him, he got one of his divinity students to paint the Thirty-second Psalm on the wall opposite his bed. And that great saint descended into his dark river, singing and saying:

> O blessed is the man to whom
> Is freely pardoned
> All the transgression he hath done,
> Whose sin is covered.

> I will confess unto the Lord
>   My trespasses, said I;
> And of my sin Thou freely didst
>   Forgive the iniquity.

"Venerable Father," said Justus Jonas to Luther, when *he* was nearing *his* dark river—"Venerable Father, do you die trusting in Jesus Christ as your God and Saviour, and subscribing to the whole reformed doctrines that you constantly preached to us?" "Yes, certainly," shouted the great Reformer with his last breath. "Yes, certainly! Jesus Christ is my Lord and my God, and He is my alone Righteousness and Strength both in death as in life."

But by far and away our best handbook and guide-book as we draw near the swelling of *our* Jordan is John Bunyan's marvelous narrative of the various experiences of his puritan pilgrims as they approached the dark river, and went through it. "Now, I further saw that betwixt them and the gate above there was a river; but there was no bridge over the river; and the river was very deep. Then they addressed themselves to the water; and, entering, Christian began to sink, till he cried out to Hopeful, his neighbour, 'I sink in deep waters, the billows go over my head: all His angry waves go over me.' But Hopeful said, 'Be of good cheer, my brother, for I feel the bottom; and it is good.' And with that Christian broke out with a loud voice, 'Oh, I see Him again! and He says to me, When thou passest through the waters, I will be with thee: and through the rivers, they shall not overflow thee.'"

And some time afterward, when Christiana, the widow of Christian the pilgrim, came within sight of the same river, she called for Mr. Greatheart, her guide, and told him how matters stood with her. So he answered her that he was heartily glad for her sake, and that he could have been glad had the heavenly post come for him. Then she called for her children, and what she said to them is all to be read at the end of her fine history. The last words she was heard to say here were these: "I come, Lord, to be with Thee, and to bless Thee."

The next of that pilgrim company to come to the river was Mr. Ready-to-halt. And the last words he was heard to say were these: "Welcome life." So he also went on his way.

After this, the same post sounded his horn at the chamber door of Mr. Feeble-Mind. And his last words were: "Hold out, Faith and Patience!" And saying so, he also went over to the other side.

How Mr. Despondency and his daughter Miss Much-Afraid got over, and what they said, I leave you to read for your own desponding and much-afraid selves.

As, also, dear old Honest, and his last words. And Mr. Valiant-for-Truth, and his brave words about his sword, and about his marks and his scars that he carried over with him. And, to crown all, the magnificent speech of Mr. Standfast, than which even John Bunyan never penned two nobler pages. But how glorious it was to see how the regions beyond the dark River were all filled with horses and chariots, with pipers and with trumpeters, with singers and with players on stringed instruments, and all to welcome the pilgrims as they went up and followed one another in at the Beautiful Gate of the City. But among all John Bunyan's characters and their end, do not forget Mr. Fearing, who is in some respects the Tinker's spiritual and literary masterpiece.

And now, after all that, I will take time only to give you Bishop Butler and *his* Jordan. When the great moralist, the old Honest of the Episcopal bench, was on his deathbed, he called for his chaplain, and said to him, "Though I have endeavored to avoid sin, and to please God to the utmost of my power; yet from the consciousness of perpetual infirmities, I am still afraid to die." "My lord," said the chaplain, "you have forgotten that Jesus Christ is a Saviour." "True," said Butler, "but how shall I know that He is a Saviour for *me?*" "My lord, it is written, 'Him that cometh unto me, I will in no wise cast out.' " "True," said the bishop; "and I am surprised that though I have read that scripture a thousand times over, I never felt its virtue till this moment. And now I die happy."

Now, my brethren, let it be well understood and believed that all these dying men—from Jesus Christ Himself downward—were all but so many pioneers and forerunners to teach us how *we* are to do when we come to the swelling of our Jordan. And, first, let us learn some much-needed lessons from our Lord Himself. And especially *this* great lesson, to say at every step of our approach to our Jordan, and at every soul-sinking billow of it, "Thy will be done!" Our Lord had been saying these same sonship-words every day, and all His days; and accordingly these same sonship-words came naturally and fully and finally to His believing lips at the end of His days. For one thing, He had prayed, and that without ceasing, for thirty years, for the conversion of His unbelieving brothers and sisters at home in Nazareth. And hitherto He had prayed, as it seemed, in vain. And worse, it seemed, than in vain. For, year after year, they all seemed to go farther away from their true salvation than ever before. And yet, in all that, Christ may only have been made, more and more, like to you and to me. For years, year after year, some of you may have been praying and waiting for the true conversion of some one or more dear to you; and, like your Lord, you may have to die and to leave them as they were, only worse. And *that* may well be *the* cross of all your crosses on your deathbed.

My brethren, travelers in the Holy Land tell us that the Jordan is sometimes very mysterious, very dark, very deep, very crooked, and sometimes very angry, and without a bridge to cross it or a ford to wade it. It was so to your Lord, and it is enough for this life that the disciple be as his Lord was. My brethren, if the Son of God and the Prince of believers and your great High Priest had to say, as He looked around on His unconverted family circle, "Thy will be done," it is enough for you to be able to say the same thing. But what you are never to know here of the dark mystery of your unanswered prayer you will certainly know hereafter, even *as He now knows*.

And then Paul's old age and the nearness of his Jordan have taught many old men, and especially many old ministers, this lesson: "I am now ready to be offered, and the time of my departure is at hand. Do thy diligence therefore to come to me shortly. And bring with thee the cloak I left at Troas, and the books, and especially the parchments." And so it is with some of the successors of the book-loving Apostle. You will go into the old-age chamber of some of your ministers and you will find near their chair, and near their bed, such old-age books and such Jordan-bank books as these: John's Revelation open at the twenty-first and twenty-second chapters, and Dante's *Paradiso,* and Bunyan's *Pilgrim's Progress,* and Baxter's *Saints' Rest,* and Howe's *Blessedness of the Righteous,* and Rutherford's *Letters,* and Newman's *Dream of Gerontius,* and the *Olney* and the *Wesley Hymns.* Many years ago I went into the death chamber of an elder of this congregation, and he laid his hand on the *Westminster Confession of Faith* lying open at the great chapter on Justification, and he said to me, "Sir, I am dying in the strength of that peace-speaking chapter." Do thy diligence to bring the right books as soon as possible, wrote Paul to Timothy, his son in the Gospel.

And all men who are of a philosophic turn of mind will take *their* lesson from Bishop Butler's deathbed. "Him that cometh unto me," said the Saviour, "I will in no wise cast out."

I've read a thousand times that Scripture o'er,
Nor felt its truth till now I near the tomb:
It is enough! O Saviour Christ, I come.

"It was Bishop Butler who made me a Christian," said Dr. Chalmers to his students, generously confessing his indebtedness to the great philosopher. Let us all, like Dr. Chalmers, take the same philosopher for our everyday example —this day and every day—till we take him for our example on the last day of our earthly pilgrimage, and for our Jordanside example, and say with him: "O Lamb of God, I come."

Just as I am, without one plea
But that Thy blood was shed for me,
And that Thou bidd'st me come to Thee,
    O Lamb of God, I come.

Just as I am, and waiting not
To rid my soul of one dark blot,
To Thee, whose blood can cleanse each spot,
    O Lamb of God, I come.

Just as I am, though tossed about,
With many a conflict, many a doubt,
Fightings and fears within, without,
    O Lamb of God, I come.

Just as I am, of that free love
The breadth, length, depth, and height to prove,
Here for a season, then above,
    O Lamb of God, I come.

"And then shall the king say unto them on his right hand: Come, ye blessed of my Father, inherit the kingdom prepared for you from the foundation of the world."

And to all who so come to Him, and who keep so coming, He will surely say, "When thou passest through the waters, I will be with thee; and through the rivers, they shall not overflow thee." "Till the redeemed of the Lord shall return, and shall come to Zion with songs and with everlasting joy upon their heads: they shall obtain joy and gladness, and sorrow and sighing shall flee away."

The Nature of Angels[1]

He took not on him the nature of angels.
HEBREWS 2: 16.

"FOR UNTO the angels hath he not put in subjection the world to come, whereof we speak. But one in a certain place testified, saying, What is man, that thou art mindful of him? or the son of man, that thou visitest him? Thou madest him a little lower than the angels; thou crownedst him with glory and honour, and didst set him over the works of thy hands: thou hast put all things in subjection under his feet. For in that he put all in subjection under him, he left nothing that is not put under him. But now we see not yet all things put under him. But we see Jesus, who was made a little lower than the angels for the suffering of death, crowned with glory and honour; that he by the grace of God should taste death for every man" (Heb. 3: 5-9).

"Being made so much better than the angels, as he hath by inheritance obtained a much more excellent name than they" (Heb. 1: 4).

Why is so much made of the angels in this passage? Why is there so much space and quotation and argument expended on what seems to us a somewhat irrelevant matter? Might not the Epistle to the Hebrews have been greatly condensed and simplified had the reader's attention been fixed at once on the Priesthood of Christ instead of having to pass through this long introduction concerning angels and

[1] First given in St. George's, Edinburgh, 18th December, 1870.

Moses, which no one disputes, and which seems not to bring any strength to the great argument of the Epistle?

A slight reading of the book will suffice to start these questions, but it requires a deeper and harder reading fitly to answer them. And still such a reading will be amply repaid in a more living and intelligent hold of the main theme when we come to it.

The introductory portion of this Epistle is not addressed to mature and well-grounded Christians of the nineteenth century so much as to the immature Jewish converts of the first, who were as yet "unskillful in the word of righteousness, and had need of milk and not of strong meat." They had not yet understood the principles of the doctrine of baptism and laying on of hands, about Moses and his Law, and about angels and their place in its dispensation. The Apostle had to become all things to all men, and he knew that there was simply no use plunging at once into the heart of his theme when such obstacles as these lay in the way of his readers following him. Hence he spends several chapters on clearing the path for the weaker brethren, who feared that in going forward with the great Christian movement they were thereby somehow in danger of forsaking the old paths in which their fathers had walked.

But still the question awaits an answer. Why so much in the first and second chapters concerning angels?

The answer is simply this: the appearances and messages of angels held the place in the Old Testament that the appearance and teaching of Christ do in the New. A light surrender of the old order and the ministry of angels would have revealed but a poor capacity for receiving the new, and these Hebrews with the blood of Abraham and Isaac and Jacob, of Moses and the prophets in their veins would have their childhood steeped in Old Testament narrative concerning the deliverances wrought and the comfort sent by angels, for all down the nation's checkered history their cheering words had been heard and their ministering wing seen. And, above all, the Angel of the Covenant, the Angel of the Lord, had brought God the Father so near that it might almost be said that they had in him preludes and anticipations of the incarnation itself. It was through his ministry that the patriarchs were called, and led, and prospered; it was through his disposition of the Law that it came into Moses' hands; it was through him that the prophets spoke unto the fathers. God took the form, and came in the character, of an angel when He conveyed anything new or confirmed any old revelation of grace or truth to the Hebrew people. In a word, what the Son is under the New Testament economy, that the ministry of angels was under the Old.

But retrograde and Judaizing teachers had played on the prejudices and the piety of the Hebrew Christians by exalting Moses and the Law that came by the dispensation of angels, and, therefore, to show that Jesus is rightly counted of more honor than Moses, and that He has by indisputable inheritance a greater than an angelic name, Paul has undertaken to show that Christ has superseded the ministry of angels in revealing the Father, and also has set aside the stewardship of Moses, being a Son over His own house.

We are now ready to follow the Apostle into this argumentative passage in which he seeks to exalt the dignity of Christ above the angels.

Verse three dwells, in several striking clauses, on what the Son was, and is, and in His divine nature will ever be— the "brightness of the Father's glory, and the express image of his person, upholding all things by the word of his power." Then comes a clause covering His work on earth: "by himself he purged our sins," and then another stating that He is now "at the right hand of the Majesty on high."

Verse four, then, accounts for His exaltation, and so carries forward the arguments for this excellent dignity of the risen Redeemer. He has sat down at the right hand of God, "being made so much better than the angels, as he hath by inheritance obtained a more excellent name than they."

This passage was one of the Arian strongholds during the great controversy concerning the eternal Sonship and perfect divinity of the Redeemer. This verse was taken along with the second verse of the third chapter, in which it is said that Christ was "faithful to him that appointed or made him," and also, Acts 2: 36, in which Peter says: "Therefore let all the house of Israel know assuredly, that God hath made that same Jesus, whom ye have crucified, both Lord and Christ." In those passages, as here, the word "made" plainly occurs concerning the Saviour. And that fact kept these verses like so many disputed provinces which were taken and retaken by Arian and Orthodox till Athanasius finally settled the sense of these texts and put into the great creed that the Son was "begotten not made." But how did he and his followers get over the plain words of the text? How is the Arian sound shown to contain an orthodox sense?

In this way and from the plain text of Scripture. The Son who was in the form of God, or, as here, the "express image of his person," and who "thought it no robbery to be equal with God, made himself of no reputation, and took upon him the form of a servant": the maker of all was made in the likeness of men, being made of a woman, and made under the Law. And being found in fashion as a man, He yet further humbled Himself, and became obedient unto death, even the death of the Cross. Wherefore God hath highly exalted Him, and given Him a name that is above every name, a more excellent name than angel ever bore. For "at the name of Jesus every knee shall bow, and every tongue confess that Jesus Christ is Lord to the glory of God the Father."

The Arians understood not His generation; because He

was "found in fashion as a man," His eternal life was denied. They staggered at the grace of the incarnation. The mystery of godliness, God manifest in the flesh, was too deep for them. For remaining what He was, the eternal Son, He became what He was not, the Son of man, and of the seed of Abraham. In being made man, He "was made a little lower than the angels," and those spiritual beings whom He created by His own power actually came and ministered unto Him after His temptation in the wilderness, and strengthened Him in His agony in the Garden. But though He has thus emptied Himself, though He has thus for our salvation become what He was not, still He necessarily remains what He was, Son of God. Conditions change, relations hold. He is Son of God made Son of man; He is Son still, though Son incarnate, and in a temporary state of suffering and emptiness and humiliation. Here, then, is a condition of things that makes it plain why Scripture should fearlessly say about its divine Lord, that He was made Lord and Christ, having been "faithful to him that appointed him," that having finished His work the Father raised Him from the dead, and gave Him back His glory, and made Him so much higher than the angels, as he originally, and prior to His humiliation, had a much more excellent name than they.

At the resurrection and exaltation of Christ He was but putting on again that glory He had for our service put off; when He sat down on the right hand of God He was but repossessing Himself of a place and an honor that were inalienably and eternally His own.

But there is more room still for the correct phrase, "made so much better than the angels," for it is not only the Son resuming His suspended honor, and returning to His sonship seat; but He is returning in a new character, and in a form that shows the Father's grace to be as great in the exaltation of Christ as the Son's grace was shown to be great in His voluntary humiliation. For the Son is returning to the Father's throne, the Father's bosom, not only divine Son still, but Son of man in addition. It is a new honor and experience to the Son, and a new display of grace is to realize that He should re-enter to the most excellent glory as a man. It is true that the assumption of the human nature into the divine glory in heaven was an easy and a natural thing after its assumption into the Sonship on earth, that it drew the rest naturally, necessarily after it. Hence this is no empty apotheosis of a man, but a far more wonderful and gracious work, the incarnation of the Son of God and His subsequent reinstallation into all the Sonship rights and prerogatives. He took our nature, in it purged our sins, and then returned whence He had come, went back to the Father with whom He had been before the world was. Thus the exaltation is not of the divine nature only, nor is it a deification of the human only. It is the exaltation of that divine Person who is now God-Man. It is the answer to the Son's prayer, "Glorify thou me with the glory which I had with thee before the world was," before I had emptied myself that I might glorify Thee.

It was a new thing on the earth that the eternal Son of God should tabernacle among men, purging their sins; and it was a new thing in heaven that a son of man should appear at the right hand of the Majesty on high. For this man whom the Jews crucified is assuredly now made Lord Christ. And He is as high above angels as a lord is above his dependents, as the son is above the servants. And they are ever confessing it. When He had finished the work that was given Him to do, when He had purged our sins, and burst the bonds of death, and blessed His disciples, and sent them to wait on the Spirit's descent, earth had no more work for Him to do. And He turned His face to His Father's house. That hour there rang a shout through heaven, the like of which had not been heard there since the morning stars sang together—the sons of God shouted for joy at the creating work of the eternal Son.

"Lift up your heads, O ye gates; even lift them up, ye everlasting doors; and the King of glory shall come in!" And as the Son passed in, and ascended to His Father's presence, the angels looking on might have said, "He is preferred before us, for He was before us." They had wondered at His surpassing grace when He had passed out into this dark and sinful world; they worshiped afresh as He passed in again, the Redeemer and Brother of fallen men.

Thus He who had so lately stood in Pilate's judgment hall with a scarlet rag on His shoulders and a crown of thorns on His head, and a reed in His hand, and a crowd of rude men paying Him mock homage till the hour should come to crucify Him, now compels the deep worship of the highest heavens as He enters with glory as the Lamb that has been slain, having on His vesture and on His thigh a name written more excellent than that of any angel—King of kings and Lord of lords.

And a voice was heard in heaven saying, "Sit thou at my right hand until I make thine enemies thy footstool. . . . Thy throne is for ever and ever. . . . Ask of me and I will give thee the heathen for thine inheritance, and the uttermost parts of the earth for thy possession." "And let all the angels of God worship him and wait on his will."

In this marvelous way the eternal Son was "made so much better than the angels, as he hath by inheritance obtained a much more excellent name than they."

But the Apostle cannot set all this as yet before his Hebrew readers. He has to walk as they are able to follow. He has to argue on premises they already accept, and quote proof and illustration from the Book they read and reverence. Hence he hitches himself to the Old Testament and goes to work to prove by lengthened and full quotation that the Messiah promised there, the Messiah promised to and expected by the fathers, was one who confessedly had a more excellent name than the angels or than Moses. The prophecy that came by the mouth of angels gave to the coming One a name and work far higher than their own. They came and spoke as witnesses and heralds of a greater than any prophet or king who had yet arisen.

Now, the Hebrew Christians confessed that Jesus was the Messiah, that all the Messianic promises and expectations were fulfilled, or were yet to be fulfilled, in Him. And the Apostle, to disarm their doubt, and allay their discomfort, about the place the Old was getting in the triumph of the New, shows them that the New is the triumph of the Old, that Jesus who is the Messiah has simply got that which was promised to the Messiah. That His name and rank are higher than the angels that it might be fulfilled that was spoken in Moses and the fathers and in the prophets concerning Him. "Come, open your Scriptures," he says, "and I will show you that that Old Testament—book and economy—you are so jealous for gives such a name and place to the Messiah as my doctrine gives to Him whom you confess to be the Messiah."

Hence the long quotations that fill the page and lay a deep and broad Messianic foundation for this weighty Epistle. But the method of proof that an inspired writer drew out to satisfy the minds and settle the heart of an ancient Christian fails, it seems, to satisfy and settle the modern rationalist. The Apostle's exegesis yields dogmatic results that are distasteful and inadmissible, and therefore his scholarship, his intelligence, his inspiration, and even his literary honesty are boldly questioned and impugned. And the narrow, irrational canon is laid down, even by theological teachers, that we are to "read Scripture and quote it like any other book."

If this is admitted, of course there is an end, if not of religious sentiment and moral duty, at least of all defined and trustworthy theology, as well as of much of the peculiar edification and comfort obtained from Holy Scripture. The believer and the rationalist thus part company at the very threshold of the question. The Christian cannot read Scripture as he reads another book, because for him no other book can claim such an author, as no other book raises such questions, or claims or commands such a hearing. As the Book itself says: "The letter killeth, but the Spirit giveth life." A literal, rationalistic interpretation kills all life out of the Psalms and Prophets, just as a devout and spiritual reading getteth life and giveth it.

Many questions connected with the principles on which New Testament writers quote from and allude to in the Old are raised and discussed in view of this passage before us. But they are more suited to the study and the classroom than to the pulpit. Still, before looking at these quotations in passing, it may be useful to some to say a word on the general relation that holds between the first volume of Holy Scripture and the second, between the Psalms and Prophets on the one hand and the Gospels and Epistles on the other.

There is nothing in the literary history of the world at all to compare with the Bible viewed purely on its literary side. A succession of writers has arisen for many generations of men and in lands far separated in place and circumstance from each other, and produced a book with beginning, middle, and end, a book which is one in plan and doctrine, and aim and spirit, though it deals with the most difficult and lofty questions, and though scholars and poets and orators, craftsmen and fishermen and plowmen have contributed to its contents. Take it at the close of any of its divisions, at the close of the Pentateuch, at the close of the Psalms, at the close of the Prophets—the book is complete, but it is as a seed or a bud is complete. It is perfect for its stage, but its stage is one of growth and maturity.

Read Moses and the Prophets and you cannot fail to see that the Old Testament is one in this, that whoever is the writer or the speaker, the spirit of the book, the attitude of the religious life, is one of expectancy and outlook.

The old stands ever on tiptoe looking for the rising of the new, holding forth empty hands, empty but for the typical washing they celebrate and the prophetic words they hold. They rejoice in God and in what He has done, but they feel that His best waits to be done, and they rejoice with the chastened joy of sojourners and strangers who feel that without us they are not to be made perfect. On one page the Prophet is so lifted up in hope and faith that a thousand years are as one day; he seems to see the day of the Lord and his hope is made glad; turn it and a day of sorrow has fallen, and he is crying, "How long, O Lord, how long?"

The Messianic prophecies are like the garden of the Lord, but it is early summer there; it is rich with buds and blossoms, it is not yet the time of fruit-bearing. The day of the Lord comes and the buds burst in His presence. The fullness of time has brought the fulfilling of prophecy and the unlocking of the type. And still the Book must be read according to its own laws, and not as another book. Even when prophecy is fulfilled and the antitype has come, still He is found to speak another language than the wise men and princes of this world know. He still speaks in words which the Holy Ghost teacheth, which are to one man foolishness, to another the wisdom of God, because by Him they were spiritually discovered. "Open thou mine eyes, O God, that I may behold wondrous things out of thy law."

The New Testament preacher or writer may be not unfitly likened to a man thinking or writing in a language he is both learning and adding to as he writes. In the construction of an argument like this the Apostle is like one seeking a fit word to clothe his thought so as to place both before his readers. Yea, the thought will not shape itself aright till the right word comes, till the old figure and illustration are found that at once embody it fully and shed light on it clearly. As he recalls and sets down in order those quotations, he knows that they will set forth with authority as well as perspicacity what is struggling in his mind. This habit of leaning on the past, and drawing strength from it, even when they were going far beyond it, is as characteristic of the prophets as it is of the apostles. David and Isaiah are the scholars of Moses; they quote from, expound, and apply him just as our Apostle here quotes and applies them. And the books then appear as at once grafted on and growths out of one another.

To change the figure, the rich, golden threads of Messianic prophecy are visible from the beginning of the web, though they do not find their end and design till the figure rises in the middle of the work into which they enter, to be lost in its wealth and beauty. And the Apostle here but traces some of the brightest and strongest of such threads up through the loom to prove that the original design had contemplated and made provision for such a central figure.

He is but in his way doing what Christ Himself did when teaching the reluctant disciples concerning the old intention of His suffering and His glory. "These are the things I said unto you while I was yet with you, that all things must be fulfilled which were written in the law of Moses, and in the prophets, and in the psalms concerning me." Thus opened He the understanding of the Hebrew Christians to both the Messiahship and the Sonship of Jesus. For He who was eternal Son, when He had purged our sins, sat down again at the right hand of God, being made so much better than the angels as He hath by inheritance, and even by Jewish prophecy, a much more excellent name than they. "For," he goes on to quote from the Hebrew Scriptures, "to which of the angels said the Father at any time,

Thou art my Son, this day have I begotten thee?" **Now,** He said this to the Messiah in prophecy.

And, again, when the Father bringeth the First-begotten into the world He saith: "He maketh his angels spirits and his ministers a flame of fire." And, again, quoting from the great Messianic Psalms, the Apostle proves that the coming One is then addressed as possessing just such royal dignity and state as Jesus is now advanced to. Indeed, we search in vain in the historical and doctrinal books of the New Testament for a richer and more exact statement of the Son's glory and reward than we find here in a prophetic psalm concerning the Messiah. "Thy throne, O righteousness is the sceptre of thy kingdom. Thou hast loved righteousness and hated iniquity; therefore God, even thy God, hath anointed thee with oil of gladness above thy fellows."

The psalm from which the Apostle quotes next is not usually looked on as properly a Messianic psalm, but he finds language there that he knows his readers must admit to be applicable to the Son, as he and they are at one that the Son created the worlds: "Thou Lord in the beginning hast laid the foundation of the earth; and the heavens are the works of thine hands: they shall perish; but thou remainest; and they all shall wax old as doth a garment; and as a vesture worn out, and to be laid aside, shalt thou fold them up, and they shall be changed: but thou art the same, and thy years shall not fail!"

In a word, to come back to the original thought, "To which of the angels has the Father said at any time, Sit on my right hand till I make thine enemies thy footstool?" The question more than answers itself, for, confessedly, the angels are but ministering spirits sent forth from the Son's throne to minister to those He has redeemed, to those who are to be heirs of salvation.

Of this argument and proof, this, then, is the sum: He is

Son, in His incarnation and exalted state, Son of God, and angels are His ministers and messengers.

By these quotations and references the Apostle proves what he has advanced above, that the Son is higher than the highest of creatures, better by so much as His inherited name was better than theirs. He is Son and heir; they are servants and ministers of His.

But His name has an excellency above that of inheritance. He inherits a great name from His Father, but He adds fresh glory to His name as the ages roll on.

He is Son by nature, but He is Creator and Redeemer. He is the Messiah of the Old Testament and the Jesus of the New, a sacrifice on earth and a great High Priest in heaven. By grace He has won those names as by His sword alone, and added them to that of Son. But that original, inherited name is the ground and basis of all, just as His divine nature underlies His human and all that in it He performs. He went forth as Son to make all things; He was set forth as Son to inherit man. As Son of God He came forth from the Father to be the brightness of His glory and the express image of His person, and as Son of God and Son of man He himself purged our sins. But in all these He got Him glory, and now He has a name written so full, so deep, so rich with gracious significance that hitherto no man knoweth it but He Himself. But that rich name He now bears will be opened up and put on the lips of His people when they are finally with Him to behold His eternal glory as Son and His added glory as Saviour. But, meantime, His excellent name grows as His work grows, and as His heirship falls in, as in our names a new syllable added may be to the initiated a hint of a whole family history. An ancestry of wealth and honor may be claimed and conceded, and a rich inheritance held by a few letters added to a personal name. Thus ancient names are not seldom made up of fragments of history: they are badges of rank, and signs of heirship and possession. Thus it is that when He shall in heaven or on earth have finished the work His Father and His brethren have given Him to do, He is to be brought forth to the eyes of His people and is to be greeted by the names Faithful and True, not indeed for the first time, but for the first time in all their fullness and warmth on our lips; and on His head shall be many crowns, and He shall have a name written that no man has hitherto known but He Himself:

> Jesus, my Lord! I know His name,
> His name is all my boast:
> Nor will He put my soul to shame,
> Nor let my hope be lost.
> Then will He own His servant's name
> Before His Father's face,
> And in the New Jerusalem
> Appoint my soul a place.

The full knowledge of His name is too wonderful for you. The deep things hidden in it are past finding out. Your heart loses the awful thrill that runs through it as you hear that He is the brightness of His Father's glory and the express image of His person; but surely your sin and need will not let you forget what the Angel of the Lord said to Joseph: "Thou shalt call his name Jesus, for he shall save his people from their sins."

One Thing Thou Lackest[1]

MARK 10: 21

IT IS NOT for a moment to be supposed that our Lord took this young man at his own estimate of himself. It is a fine instance of our Lord becoming all things to all men when He stops on His way to listen to this young man talk to him about this commandment and that commandment in this artless fashion. Nobody who knows anything about the commandments, and about themselves, can but smile over this young man's innocence, guilelessness, and simplicity. "Good Master, all these things have I observed from my youth up." And Jesus beholding him, loved him. And so do we. We love a child so long as he speaks as a child, and understands as a child, and thinks as a child. But, after today, this young man will remain a child no longer. From today this young man will, all at once, have become an old man. From today his besetting sin will have found him out. From today his far too early love of money will be the root of all evil to him. And it was because our Lord saw all that was in that young man's heart and foresaw all that young man's future life, and the end of it all, that He beheld him, and loved him, and said to him, "One thing thou lackest."

1. Now, had this young man been able to bear it, our

[1] This sermon was one in a series entitled "Our Lord's Teaching," and is No. VII. Preached in Free St. George's Church, Edinburgh, on May 5th, 1895. The order of worship included the *reading* of Mark 10: 13-41 and Philippians 3: 4-14 and the *singing* of Psalm 103: 13-18, Anthem No. 12, Psalm 147: 1-5, Hymn No. 187, Hymn No. 178, vs. 2-4, Psalm 90: 14-17.

Lord would have spoken to him in the language of the Apostle, would have told him that the one thing he lacked was that the whole law of God, and every single commandment of it, should enter his heart like a two-edged sword. But our Lord would not have been understood had He so spoken that day, and so it was that He took this direct, practical, and unmistakable way of dealing with the innocent and ignorant youth. It is all but certain that the Apostle had this young man in his mind when he was engaged on his Epistle to the Romans, and when in that Epistle he wrote this concerning himself: "I was alive without the law once," and to the Galatians: "And I profited in the Jews' religion above many my equals in mine own nation, being more exceeding zealous of the traditions of my fathers," and to the Philippians: "An Hebrew of the Hebrews; as touching the law, a Pharisee; as touching the righteousness which is in the law, blameless."

"But when the commandment came," *came home, that is,* sin revived, and I died. Wherefore the law is holy, and just, and good." Paul made a tremendous fight against the law entering his heart. He welcomed the letter of the law, that is, as a guide to conduct but not to conscience, and, indeed, boasted of it, and of himself because of it. He "profited" by it above all his equals in his own nation. The law at one time was Paul's very life; it was his confidence and his crown so long as he kept it out of his heart. "Master, all these things have I kept blamelessly from my youth up." But when, in his own experimental word, "the law *entered,*" then *all* his legal ceremonies, and all his traditional observances, and all his surface moralities gave way, and went down before the holiness, the justice, the goodness, the spirituality, and the exquisite inwardness of the law of God, till, in his own marked and perfect word, he *died—died daily,* and lay dead every day till he was again brought to life by the grace of God and by the Spirit of

Christ. And let us hope that this young Pharisee also came, as life went on, to something of Paul's depth of mind, and tenderness of conscience, and holiness of heart. And if he did, I can hear him, as he grew in grace, and in the knowledge of his own heart and of the law of God—I can hear him saying with a sigh of shame and a smile of scorn at himself: "When I was a child, I spake as a child, I understood as a child, I thought as a child." Now, how do *you* stand, not to this or that commandment, not to adultery, or murder, or theft, or false witness, or fraud, but to the spirituality and the holiness and the splendid inwardness of all the commandments? "For the word of God is quick and powerful, and sharper than any two-edged sword, piercing even to the dividing asunder of soul and spirit and of the joints and marrow, and is a discerner of the thoughts and intents of the heart."

2. And, then, after that, the "one thing" that Paul had lacked, and now received anew of God every day, and preached and wrote on every day, was this, that the *law was abolished and abrogated under the gospel.* The whole law of Moses, and all the zealous traditions that the fathers had heaped on the law of Moses—all these things were completely fulfilled and forever abolished by the coming of Christ. And not the ceremonial law only, but even the moral law, even the Ten Commandments, even the holy, and just, and good, and perfect law of God—even *it* was completely abrogated and forever abolished out of the whole sphere and region of justification and forgiveness of sin. Paul, with all his magnificent gifts of mind, and with all his unparalleled penetration into the nature of law, the nature of sin, the nature of grace, and the nature of gospel peace and gospel holiness—Paul was raised up, and equipped, and sent out, and was sustained and supported to the end, that he might preach and write to all time, and till time should be no longer, the absolute abrogation and the utter abolish-

ment of the whole law of God, so far as the believing sinner's justification is concerned. Paul's Epistle to the Romans is, in this respect, the topstone and masterpiece of the whole Book of God. Read in it every day, read your guilty conscience deepening in it every day, for it is the written-out and sealed-up charter of your blood-bought peace with God. And then pass on to *Galatians,* which is a right noble codicil, complement, reinforcement and finish of the great *Romans,* till, when you have understanding and skill to take those two Epistles together, you will "lack" nothing of the full assurance of your peace with God, and your joy in God through your Lord and Saviour Jesus Christ.

These, then, are *two* things, the *two foundation things,* that we all "lack" the full knowledge of—*first,* the entrance of the law of God into our hearts, so that the offense of our hearts may abound; and then, second, when sin abounds, first then does grace much more abound; there grace reigns, through righteousness, unto eternal life through Jesus Christ our Lord. But while the whole law of God is forever abrogated and abolished to the penitent and believing sinner in the grand matter of his *justification,* it is so far from being abolished, or abrogated or in any degree suspended for his *sanctification,* that it puts on, for that end, a quite new, and a hitherto undiscovered, strength, and depth, and inwardness, and quick spirituality under the Gospel. "A new commandment I give unto you," says our Lord to us. And that "new commandment" runs out into ramifications, and refinements, and subtleties, and sensibilities in the spiritual mind, and in the holy heart, past all description and past all belief. And, he performs to us a service only second to Paul's service to us in *Romans* and in *Galatians,* who assist us either in his pulpit or by his pen,—*first,* to the *knowledge,* and then to the *attainment* of the things we still "lack," in the keeping, and in the cleansing of our hearts, and in the perfecting and the finishing of our moral character, and in the blamelessness and the beauty of our walk and conversation before God and man.

3. There is "one thing" we all "lack," my brethren, both the justified and those still under condemnation, and all our other lacks come from that lack: we all "lack" *love*. That "new commandment" has not yet entered our hearts. If it had, we would be perfect men, lacking nothing. He who has *love,* and *enough love,* against him there is no law. But *what,* in this respect, *is love?* Well, *love* is just *love.* Love is never anything else but just *love.* Love is love everywhere, and wherever love is it fulfills the whole law. Love worketh no ill to his neighbor. Love suffereth long, and is kind. Love envieth not. Love seeketh not his own. Love beareth all things. Against love like that there is no law. For love is the fulfilling of *all* law. Now, love like that is the "one thing" lacking in us all. Many also lack even the very *idea* of such love. They lack the very *visual image* of it. They have never begun to *imagine* what it would be to themselves, and to their neighbors to have a heart like that. They are destroyed for lack of imagination, and then for lack of heart. Only, they do not know their destruction. He knows only his dreadful and self-destructive lack of love who carries about the law of it, and who endeavors after it in his heart, and in his imagination, and in his conscience every day and toward every man. O wretched man that I am, he cries, who shall fill me full of the life of love? How shall I be made a partaker of the Divine Nature! I thank God through Jesus Christ my Lord.

4. And then there are many men in every community who totally "lack" that which is next to love in its indispensableness,—they totally lack *character*. It is as impossible to define as to describe *love* aright, though we all know quite well what love is. And it is as impossible to define or describe *character,* though we all recognize its presence and at once feel its absence. A man will have birth, talent,

station, religion even, and will yet totally lack character. No good man respects the man who lacks character; he fain would, but he cannot. No bad man fears the man who lacks character. The man who lacks character—his very children begin to find him out to their shame and confusion of face, and his best friends shrink from the task of defending him. It is an awful, and an almost hopeless, sentence to pass on any man to say that he totally lacks character. And yet, if only he could see it; if only he would accept it, and set about it, even the man who is today totally without intellectual, or moral, or religious character—there is no limit to what he might attain in that noblest and most lasting of all attainments, *moral* character. And the more astonished out of measure, saying among themselves, who then can be saved? And Jesus looking on them said, With men it is impossible, but not with God, for with God all things are possible.

5. There is nothing—it is much to be suspected—but, let each man answer for himself, only it is much to be feared that there is anything that is more lacking among us, after love, than a *life of prayer*. As His teaching and preaching gathered to an end our Lord became more and more anxious about His disciples in the matter of prayer. His last recorded conversation with His disciples turned almost wholly on prayer, till it ended in that amazing prayer that must have carried their cold hearts captive to sit still and hear it. My brethren, I am bold to say to all your faces that you are all shamefully and scandalously lacking in prayer, criminally lacking in prayer for your households, for your friends, and for all men. You scamp and hurry over, and stint prayer till your neglect of prayer is the secret source of all your other sins and omissions. You look askance at secret prayer as if there was a yoke in it, and a cross, and a task, and a bondage. You measure out the moments. You say, "That will do." You say that you have done well

enough tonight. You lack the whole spirit, and genius, and taste, and relish, and heavenly joy of prayer. And, lacking the spirit and the habit of prayer, you lack everything.

6. And, in connection with that, I will wager that one good long pew would hold all the communicants in this congregation, who, on system, and on conscience, pass every fast day under a strict scrutiny before they lie down to sleep. You lack a mighty instrument for the working out of your salvation, you who neglect a strict, a solemn, and a penitential self-examination at the close of every day. The wise merchantman will write up his books every night. He will go over all the gains and all the losses of the past day. "Has this been a good day with me, or a bad? How does this day compare with the good and the bad of yesterday? What have I to say, and do, before God before I can safely lie down and lose myself in sleep tonight? How did I get through that hour of temptation today? How did I get through that trial of temper, and that trial of patience, and that trial of humility and meekness, and that trial of self-mastery and self-denial? What fatal "lack," then, must be in that man's whole religion, and what a fatal danger to his eternal salvation, who has no time at night to repent of the past day! How that man can expect to put off his old sins, and to put on Christ, I cannot imagine. I much fear he never does, and never will, till he wholly alters his last hours every night and his first hour every morning. He is a brave man, and he must have a lease of life, who can lie down to sleep, night after night, year in and year out, without repentance, and without prayer, and without the sprinkling of the blood of Christ! This is to be said for such a man, that he is a bold man, and is not afraid.

7. *He* who so examines himself, *he* who so recalls and reviews every past day—*he* will not need any preacher to tell him what he lacks. His own broken heart will preach to him every late night and every early morning, aye, and

all through his busiest day, till it would be a fine thing to get that man up into the pulpit to preach to us on the one thing that he and we still lack. I can see him; I can hear him as he speaks to us about all the things still lacking in his own heart and life, and in ours. Now, it would be our total lack of love, and now our total lack of character, now our lack of prayer, and now our lack of that fountainhead of prayer—our self-examination every night. One night he would be so bitter at himself for his lack of patience and longsuffering all the past day with the unthankful and the evil; another night his bad temper all that day would make his head waters, and then, another day, something happens to him that fills his heart full—till there is no more room in it—full of suspicion, and resentment, and retaliation, and revenge. Such a man will feel that he lacks any right to pray for the forgiveness of his debts by either God or man. There is this also that we all lack, some less and some more, the *will* and the *ability* to put ourselves in other people's places, so as to ask at all times, How would I like that said and done to me? *This, also,* is too much lacking among us, a wise and a constant attention to our children in their little morals, manners, in their little behavior, and in their prayers. But, at this rate, where are we to stop? Well may we exclaim, "Who, then, at this rate, can be saved?" And yet, all the time, there is no salvation there of all that. *That is* salvation. There is nothing else to be called salvation. Salvation is a snare and a deception where it is not all that, and far more than all that. O God of salvation, O God with whom such a salvation is possible, save us with this great, and full, and free, and everlasting salvation!

8. Now, it may very well be that in all this I have not come within a thousand miles of the "one thing" that you "lack." But you know that so sorely lacking thing yourself. Your own conscience knows it. God within you knows it. Nay, He knows it who spake about it that day to that

young man. What you "lack" is between Jesus Christ your Judge and you, and no one else has any business with it. Deal with Him, then, about it. Do not go away from Him "sad," as the young man went away about it. Do not be "grieved" as he was about it. Do not say, Who, then, can be saved with a "lack" like mine? Do not say that your salvation with such a lack is impossible. So it is, but not with God. And God is on your side from that moment when you resolve to deal with your one thing lacking. All things are possible with God, aye, and with you, as soon as you turn to God. Turn to Him, then. Turn to Him now. Tell Him what you lack, and for how long you have lacked it, till you are hopeless about it. And, no sooner will you have so turned and so said then He will, from that moment, receive you, and assist you, and relieve you. And from that moment, a new life, a redeemed and a delivered life, will begin within you. You will from that day have a good conscience toward God, and toward yourself, and half the battle stands in that. And you will, from that day, have a new courage and a new hope about yourself. And it will give you also what you have not had for long, what, indeed, you *never* had before—an object and an aim in life worth living for, and worth laboring for, and worth fighting for. And, as life goes on, and as the things you still "lack" seem to multiply on you, as they will, and seem to deepen within you, as they will—all that will only throw you back, with a new understanding, and with a new heart, on Paul's noble confession, and noble resolution, so nobly expressed: "Not as though I had already attained, either were already perfect: brethren, I count not myself to have apprehended: but this one thing I do, I press toward the mark for the prize of the high calling of God in Christ Jesus."

The Interpreter

An interpreter, one among a thousand.
JOB 33: 23.

We come tonight to the Interpreter's House. And since every minister of the Gospel is an interpreter, and every evangelical church is an interpreter's house, let us gather up some of the precious lessons to ministers and to people with which this passage of the *Pilgrim's Progress* so much abounds.

1. In the first place, then, I observe that the House of the Interpreter stands just beyond the Wicket Gate. In the whole topography of the *Pilgrim's Progress* there lies many a deep lesson. The church that Mr. Worldly-Wiseman supported, and on the communion roll of which he was so determined to have our pilgrim's so unprepared name, stood far down on the other side of Goodwill's gate. It was a fine building, and it had an eloquent man for its minister, and the whole service was an attraction and an enjoyment to all the people of the place. But our Interpreter was never asked to show any of his significant things there; and, indeed, neither minister nor people would have understood him had he ever done so. And had any of the parishioners from below the gate ever by any chance stumbled into the Interpreter's house, his most significant rooms would have had no significance to them. Both he and his house would have been a mystery and an offense to Worldly-Wiseman, his minister, and his fellow worshipers. John Bunyan has the clear warrant of both Jesus Christ and the Apostle Paul

for the place on which he has planted the Interpreter's house. "It is given to you," said our Lord to His disciples, "to know the mysteries of the kingdom of heaven, but to them it is not given." And Paul tells us that "the natural man receiveth not the things of the Spirit of God, for they are foolishness unto him: neither can he know them, because they are spiritually discerned." And, accordingly, no reader of the *Pilgrim's Progress* will really understand what he sees in the Interpreter's House unless he is already a man of a spiritual mind. Intelligent children enjoy the pictures and the people set before them in this illustrative house, but they must become the children of God, and must be well on in the life of God, before they will be able to say that the house next the gate has been a profitable and a helpful house to them. All that is displayed here—all the furniture and all the vessels, all the ornaments and all the employments and all the people of the Interpreter's House—is fitted and intended to be profitable as well as interesting to pilgrims only. No man has any real interest in the things of this house, or will take any abiding profit out of it, till he is fairly started on the upward road. In his former life, and while still on the other side of the gate, our pilgrim had no interest in such things as he is now to see and hear; and if he had seen and heard them in his former life, he would not, with all the Interpreter's explanation, have understood them. As here among ourselves tonight, they who will understand and delight in the things they hear in this house are only those who have really begun to live a religious life. The realities of true religion are now the most real things in life to them; they love divine things now; and since they began to love divine things, you cannot entertain them better than by exhibiting and explaining divine things to them. There is no house in all the earth, after the gate itself, that is more dear to the true pilgrim heart than the Interpreter's House. "I was glad when it was said to me, Let us go into the house of the Lord. Peace be within thy walls, and prosperity within thy palaces."

2. And besides being built on the very best spot in all the land for its owner's purposes, every room in that great house was furnished and fitted up for the entertainment and instruction of pilgrims. Every inch of that capacious and many-chambered house was given up to the delectation of pilgrims. The public rooms were thrown open for their convenience and use at all hours of the day and night, and the private rooms were kept retired and secluded for such as sought retirement and seclusion. There were dark rooms also, with iron cages in them, till Christian and his companions came out of those terrible places, bringing with them an everlasting caution to watchfulness and a sober mind. There were also rooms given up to vile and sordid uses. One room there was full of straws and sticks and dust, with an old man who did nothing day or night but wade about among the straws and sticks and dust, and rake them all into little heaps, and then sit watching lest any one should overturn them. And then, strange to tell, and not easy to get to the full significance of it, the bravest room in all the house had absolutely nothing in it but a huge, ugly, poisonous spider hanging to the wall with her feet. "Is there but one spider in all this spacious room?" asked the Interpreter. And the water stood in Christiana's eyes; she also had come by this time thus far on her journey. She was a woman of quick apprehension, and the water stood in her eyes at the Interpreter's question, and she said: "Yes, Lord, there is here more than one. Yea, and spiders whose venom is far more destructive than that which is in her." The Interpreter then looked pleasantly on her, and said, "Thou hast said the truth." This made Mercy blush, and the boys to cover their faces, for they all began now to understand the riddle. "This is to show you," said the Interpreter, "that however full of the venom of sin you may be,

yet you may, by the hand of faith, lay hold of, and dwell in, the best room that belongs to the King's House above." Then they all seemed to be glad, but the water stood in their eyes. A wall also stood apart on the grounds of the house with an always dying fire on one side of it, while a man on the other side of the wall continually fed the fire through hidden openings in the wall. A whole palace also stood on the grounds, the inspection of which so kindled our pilgrim's heart that he refused to stay here any longer, or to see any more sights—so much had he already seen of the veil of sin and of the blessedness of salvation. Not that he had seen as yet the half of what that house held for the instruction of pilgrims. Only, time would fail us to visit the hen and her chickens, the butcher killing a sheep and pulling her skin over her ears, and she lying still under his hands and taking her death patiently; also the garden with the flowers all diverse in stature, and quality, and color, and smell, and virtue, and some better than some, and all where the gardener had set them, there they stand, and quarrel not with one another. The robin redbreast also, so pretty of note and color and carriage, but, instead of bread and crumbs, and such like harmless matter, with a great spider in his mouth. A tree also, whose inside was rotten, and yet it grew and had leaves. So they went on their way and sang:

> This place hath been our second stage,
>   Here have we heard and seen
> Those good things that from age to age
>   To others hid have been.
>
> The butcher, garden, and the field,
>   The robin and his bait,
> Also the rotten tree, doth yield
>   Me argument of weight;
>
> To move me for to watch and pray,
>   To strive to be sincere,

> To take my cross up day by day,
> And serve the Lord with fear.

The significant rooms of that divine house instruct us also that all the lessons requisite for our salvation are not to be found in any one scripture or in any one sermon, but that all that is required by any pilgrim or any company of pilgrims should all be found in every minister's ministry as he leads his flock on from one Sabbath day to another, rightly dividing the word of truth. Our ministers should have something in their successive sermons for everybody. Something for the children, something for the slow-witted and the dull of understanding, something especially suited for those who are of a quick apprehension; something at one time to make the people smile, at another time to make them blush, and at another time to make the water stand in their eyes.

3. And then the Interpreter's life was as full of work as his house was of entertainment and instruction. Not only so, but his life, it was well known, had been quite as full of work before he had a house to work for as ever it had been since. The Interpreter did nothing but continually preside over his house and all that was in it and around, and it was all gone over and seen to with his own eyes and hands every day. He had been present at the laying of every stone and beam of that solid and spacious house of his. There was not a pin or a loop of its furniture, there was not a picture on its walls, not a bird or a beast in its woods and gardens, that he did not know all about and could not hold discourse about. And then, after he had taken you all over his house, with its significant rooms and woods and gardens, he was full all suppertime of all wise saws and witty proverbs. "One leak will sink a ship," he said that night, "and one sin will destroy a sinner." And all their days the pilgrims remembered that word from the Interpreter's lips,

and they often said it to themselves as they thought of their own besetting sin. Now, if it is indeed so, that every Gospel minister is an interpreter, and every evangelical church an interpreter's house, what an important passage this is for all those who are proposing and preparing to be ministers.

Let them reflect on it: what a house this is that the Interpreter dwells in; how early and how long ago he began to lay out his grounds and to build his house on them; how complete in all its parts it is, and how he still watches and labors to have it more complete. Understandest thou what thou here readest? It is asked of all ministers, young and old, as they turn over John Bunyan's pungent pages. And every new room, every new bird, and beast, and herb, and flower makes us blush for shame as we contrast our own insignificant and ill-furnished house with the noble house of the Interpreter. Let all our students who have not yet fatally destroyed themselves and lost their opportunity lay the Interpreter's House well to heart. Let them be students, not in idle name only, as so many are, but in intense reality, as so few are. Let them read everything that bears on the Bible, and let them read nothing that does not. They have not the time or the permission. Let them be content to be men of one book. Let them give themselves wholly to the interpretation of divine truth as its riddles are set in nature and in man, in scripture, in providence, and in spiritual experience. Let them store their memories at college with all sacred truth, and with all secular truth, and with all secular truth that can be made sacred. And if their memories are weak and treacherous, let them be quiet under God's will in that, and all the more labor to make up in other ways for that defect, so that they may always have something to say to the purpose when their future people come up to church hungry for instruction and comfort and encouragement. Let them look around and see the sin that sinks the ship of so many ministers; and let them begin while yet their ship is in the yard and see that she is fitted up and furnished, stored and stocked, so that she shall, in spite of sure storms and sunken rocks, deliver her freight in the appointed haven. When they are lying in bed on a Sabbath morning, let them forecast the day when they shall have to give a strict account of their eight years of golden opportunity among the churches, and the classes, and the societies, and the libraries of our university seats. Let them be able to name some great book, aye, more than one great book, they mastered, for every year of their priceless and irredeemable student life. Let them all their days have old treasure houses that they filled full with scholarship and with literature and with all that will minister to a congregation's many desires and necessities, collected and kept ready from their student days. "Meditate upon these things; give thyself wholly up to them, that thy profiting may appear unto all."

4. And then with a sly stroke at us old ministers, our significant author points out to us how much better furnished the Interpreter's House was by the time Christiana and the boys visited it compared with that early time when Christian was entertained in it. Our pilgrim got far more in the Interpreter's House of delight and instruction than he could carry out of it, but that did not tempt the Interpreter to sit down and content himself with taking all his future pilgrims in the same room, and showing them the same pictures, and repeating to them the same explanations. No, for he reflected that each coming pilgrim would need some new significant room to himself, and, therefore, as soon as he got one pilgrim off his hands he straightway set about building and furnishing new rooms, putting up new pictures, and replenishing his woods and his waters with new beasts and birds and fishes. I am ashamed, he said, that I had so little to show when I first opened my gates to receive pilgrims, and I do not know why they came to me as they did.

I was only a beginner in these things when my first visitor came to my gates. Let every long-settled, middle-aged, and even gray-headed, minister read the life of the Interpreter at this point and take courage and have hope. Let it teach us all to break some new ground in the field of divine truth with every new year. Let it teach us all to be students all our days. Let us buy, somehow, the poorest and the oldest of us, some new and first-rate book every year. Let us not, indeed, shut up altogether our old rooms if they ever had anything significant in them, but let us add now a new wing to our spiritual house, now a new picture to its walls, and now a new herb to its gardens. "Resolved," wrote Jonathan Edwards, "that as old men have seldom any advantage of new discoveries, because these are beside a way of thinking they have been long used to; resolved, therefore, if ever I live to years, that I will be impartial to hear the reasons of all pretended discoveries, and receive them, if rational, how long soever I have been used to another way of thinking."

5. The fickle, frivolous, volatile character of so many divinity students is excellently hit off by Bunyan in our pilgrim's impatience to be out of the Interpreter's House. No sooner had he seen one or two of the significant rooms than this easily satisfied student was as eager to get out of that house as he had been to get in. Twice over the wise and learned Interpreter had to beg and beseech this ignorant and impulsive pilgrim to stop and get another lesson in the religious life before he left the great schoolhouse. All our professors of divinity and all our ministers understand the parable at this point only too well. Their students are eager to get into their classes; like our pilgrim, they have heard the fame of this and that teacher, and there is not standing room in the class for the first weeks of the session. But before Christmas there is room enough for strangers, and long before the session closes, half the students are counting the weeks and plotting to petition the Assembly against the

length and labor of the curriculum. Was there ever a class that was as full and attentive at the end of the session as it was at the beginning? Never since our poor human nature was so stricken with laziness and shallowness and self-sufficiency. But what is the chaff to the wheat? It is the wheat that deserves and repays the husbandman's love and labor. When Plato looked up from his desk in the Academy, after reading and expounding one of his greatest Dialogues, he found only one student left in the classroom, but, then, that student was Aristotle. "Now let me go," said Christian. "Nay, stay," said the Interpreter, "till I have showed thee a little more." "Sir, is it not time for me to go?" "Do tarry till I show thee just one thing more."

6.   Here have I seen things rare and profitable,
        . . . Then let me be
        Thankful, O good Interpreter, to thee.

Sydney Smith, with his usual sagacity, says that the last vice of the pulpit is to be uninteresting. Now, the Interpreter's House had this prime virtue in it, that it was all interesting. Do not our children beg of us on Sabbath nights to let them see the Interpreter's show once more, it is so inexhaustibly and unfailingly interesting? It is only stupid men and women who ever weary of it. But, "profitable" was the one and universal word with which all the pilgrims left the Interpreter's House. "Rare and pleasant," they said, and sometimes "dreadful," but it was always "profitable." Now, how seldom do we hear our people at the church door step down into the street, saying, "Profitable?" If they said that oftener, their ministers would study profit more than they do. The people say "able," or "not at all able"; "eloquent," or "stammering and stumbling," "excellent" in style and manner and accent, or the opposite of all that; and their ministers, to please the people and to earn their approval, labor after these approved things. But if the people said only that the prayers and the preaching were profitable and helpful, even when they too seldom are, then our preachers would set the profit of the people far more before them, in both selecting and treating and delivering their Sabbath-day subjects. A lady on one occasion said to her minister, "Sir, your preaching does my soul good." And her minister never forgot the grace and loving look with which that was said. Not only did he never forget it, but often when selecting his subject, and treating it, and delivering it, the question would rise in his heart and conscience, Will that do my friend's soul any good? "Rare and profitable," said the pilgrim as he left the gate, and hearing that sent the Interpreter back with new spirit and new invention to fill his house of still more significant, rare, and profitable things than ever before. "Meditate on these things," said Paul to Timothy his son in the Gospel, "that thy profiting may appear unto all." "Thou art a minister of the word," wrote the learned William Perkins beside his name on all his books; "mind thy business."

The Book

. . . the book of the wars of the Lord . . .
NUMBERS 21: 14.

JOHN BUNYAN's *Holy War* was first published in 1682, six years before its illustrious author's death. Bunyan wrote this great book when he was still in all the fullness of his intellectual power and in all the ripeness of his spiritual experience. The *Holy War* is not the *Pilgrim's Progress*—there is only one *Pilgrim's Progress*. At the same time, we have Lord Macaulay's word for it that if the *Pilgrim's Progress* did not exist the *Holy War* would be the best allegory that ever was written, and even Mr. (Anthony) Froude admits that the *Holy War* alone would have entitled its author to rank high up among the acknowledged masters of English literature. The intellectual rank of the *Holy War* has been fixed before that tribunal over which our accomplished and competent critics preside; but for a full appreciation of its religious rank and value we would need to hear the glad testimonies of tens of thousands of God's saints whose hard-beset faith and obedience have been kindled and sustained by the study of this noble book. The *Pilgrim's Progress* sets forth the spiritual life under the scriptural figure of a long and an uphill journey. The *Holy War*, on the other hand, is a military history; it is full of soldiers and battles, defeats and victories. And its devout author had much more scriptural suggestion and support in the composition of the *Holy War* than he had even in the composition of the *Pilgrim's Progress*. For Holy Scripture is full of wars and rumors of wars: the wars of the Lord, the wars of Joshua and the Judges, the wars of David, with his and many other magnificent battle songs, till the best known name of the God of Israel in the Old Testament is the Lord of Hosts; and then in the New Testament we have Jesus Christ described as the Captain of our salvation. Paul's powerful use of "armor" and "armed men" is familiar to every student of his epistles; and then the whole Bible is crowned with a book all sounding with the battle cries, the shouts, and the songs of soldiers, till it ends with that city of peace where they hang the trumpet in the hall and study war no more. Military metaphors had taken a powerful hold of our author's imagination, even in the *Pilgrim's Progress,* as his portraits of Greatheart and Valiant-for-truth and other soldiers sufficiently show; while the conflict with Apollyon and the destruction of Doubting Castle are so many sure preludes of the coming *Holy War.* Bunyan's early experiences in the great Civil War had taught him many memorable things about the military art, memorable and suggestive things that he afterward put to the most splendid use in the siege, the capture, and the subjugation of Mansoul.

The *Divine Comedy* is beyond dispute the greatest book of personal and experimental religion the world has ever seen. The consuming intensity of its author's feelings about sin and holiness, the keenness and the bitterness of his remorse, and the rigor and the severity of his revenge, his superb intellect and his universal learning, all set ablaze by his splendid imagination—all that combines to make the *Divine Comedy* the unapproachable masterpiece it is. John Bunyan, on the other hand, had no learning to be called learning, but he had a strong and a healthy English understanding, a conscience and a heart wholly given up to the life of the best religion of his religious day, and then, by sheer dint of his sanctified and soaring imagination and his exquisite style, he stands forth the peer of the foremost men in the intellectual world. And thus it is that the great unlettered religious world possesses in John Bunyan all but that the select and scholarly world possesses in Dante. Both Dante and Bunyan devoted their splendid gifts to the noblest of services—the service of spiritual, and especially of personal religion; but for one appreciative reader that Dante has had Bunyan has had a hundred. Happy in being so like his Master in so many things, Bunyan is happy in being like his unlettered Master in this also, that the common people hear him gladly and never weary of hearing him.

It gives by far its noblest interest to Dante's noble book that we have Dante himself in every page of his book. Dante is taken down into Hell, he is then led up through Purgatory, and after that still up and up into the very Paradise of God. But that hell all the time is the hell that Dante had dug and darkened and kindled for himself. In the *Purgatory,* again, we see Dante working out his own salvation with fear and trembling, God all the time working in Dante to will and to do of His good pleasure. And then the Paradise, with all its sevenfold glory, is just that place and that life which God hath prepared for them that love Him and serve Him as Dante did. And so it is in the *Holy War.* John Bunyan is in the *Pilgrim's Progress,* but there are more men and other men than its author in that rich and populous book, and other experiences and other attainments than his. But in the *Holy War* we have Bunyan himself as fully and as exclusively as we have Dante in the *Divine Comedy.* In the first edition of the *Holy War* there is a frontispiece conceived and executed after the anatomical and symbolical manner which was so common in that day, and which is to be seen at its perfection in the English edition of Jacob Behmen. The frontispiece is a full-length likeness of the author of the *Holy War,* with his whole soul laid open and his hidden heart "anatomized." Why, asked Wordsworth—and Matthew Arnold in our day has echoed the question—why does Homer still so live and rule without a rival in the world of letters? And they answer that it is because he always sang with his eye so fixed on its object. "Homer, to thee I turn." And so it was with Dante. And so it was with Bunyan. Bunyan's *Holy War* has its great and abiding and commanding power over us just because he composed it with his eye fixed on his own heart.

> My readers, I have somewhat else to do,
> Than with vain stories thus to trouble you;
> What here I say some men do know so well
> They can with tears and joy the story tell. . . .
> Then lend thine ear to what I do relate,
> Touching the town of Mansoul and her state:
> For my part, I (myself) was in the town,
> Both when 'twas set up and when pulling down.
> Let no man then count me a fable-maker,
> Nor make my name or credit a partaker
> Of their derision: what is here in view,
> Of mine own knowledge, I dare say is true.

The characters in the *Holy War* are not, as a rule, nearly so clear-cut or full of dramatic life and movement as their fellows are in the *Pilgrim's Progress,* and Bunyan seems to have felt that to be the case. He shows all an author's fondness for the children of his imagination in the *Pilgrim's Progress.* He returns to and he lingers on their doings and their sayings and their very names with all a foolish father's fond delight. While, on the other hand, when we look to see him in his confidential addresses to his readers returning on some of the military and municipal characters in the *Holy War,* to our disappointment he does not so much as name a single one of them, though he dwells with all an author's self-delectation on the outstanding scenes, situations, and episodes of his remarkable book.

What, then, are some of the more outstanding scenes, situations, and episodes, as well as military and municipal characters, in the book now before us? And what are we to promise ourselves, and to expect from the study and the exposition of the *Holy War* in these lectures? Well, to begin with, we shall do our best to enter with mind, and heart, and conscience, and imagination into Bunyan's great conception of the human soul as a city, a fair and delicate city and corporation, with its situation, surroundings, privileges and fortunes. We shall then enter under his guidance into the famous and stately palace of this metropolitan city, a palace which for strength might be called a castle, for pleasantness a paradise, and for largeness a place so copious as to contain all the world. The walls and the gates of the city will then occupy and instruct us for several Sabbath evenings, after which we shall enter on the record of the wars and battles that rolled time after time around those city walls, and surged up through its captured gates till they quite overwhelmed the very palace of the king itself. Then we shall spend, God willing, one Sabbath evening with Loth-to-stoop, and another with old Ill-pause, the devil's orator, and another with Captain Anything, and another with Lord Will-be-will, and another with that notorious villain Clip-promise, by whose doings so much of the king's coin had been abused, and another with that so angry and so ill-conditioned churl old Mr. Prejudice, with his sixty deaf men under him. Dear Mr. Wet-eyes, with his rope on his head, will have a fit congregation one winter night, and Captain Self-denial another. We shall have another painful but profitable evening before a communion season with Mr. Prywell, and so we shall eat of that bread and drink of that cup. Emmanuel's livery will occupy us one evening,

Mansoul's Magna Charta another, and her annual Feastday another. Her Established Church and her beneficed clergy will take up one evening, some Skulkers in Mansoul another, the devil's last prank another, and then, to wind up with, Emmanuel's last speech and charge to Mansoul from his chariot step till He comes again to accomplish her rapture. All that we shall see and take part in, unless, indeed, our Captain comes in anger before the time, and spears us to the earth when He finds us asleep at our post or in the act of sin at it, which may His abounding mercy forbid!

And now take these three forewarnings and precautions:

1. All who come here on these coming Sabbath evenings will not understand the *Holy War* all at once, and many will not understand it at all. And little blame to them, and no wonder. For fully to understand this deep and intricate book demands far more mind, far more experience, and far more specialized knowledge than the mass of men, as men are, can possibly bring to it. This so exacting book demands of us, to begin with, some little acquaintance with military engineering and architecture, with the theory of, and if possible with some practice in, attack and defense in sieges and storms, winter campaigns and long drawn-out wars. And then, impossible as it sounds and is, along with all that we would need to have a really profound, practical, and first-hand acquaintance with the anatomy of the human subject, and especially with cardiac anatomy, as well as with all the conditions, diseases, regimen, and discipline of the corrupt heart of man. And then it is enough to terrify any one to open this book or to enter this church when he is told that if he comes here he must be ready and willing to have the whole of this terrible and exacting book fulfilled and experienced in himself, in his own body and in his own soul.

2. And then you will not all like the *Holy War*. The mass

of men could not be expected to like any such book. How could the vain and blind citizen of a vain and blind city like to be wakened up, as, Paris within our own remembrance, was wakened up to find all her gates in the hands of an iron-hearted enemy? And how could her sons like to be reminded, as they sit in their wine gardens, that they are thereby fast preparing their city for that threatened day when she is to be hung up on her own walls and bled to the white? Who would not hate and revile the book or the preacher who prophesied such rough things as that? Who could love the author or the preacher who told him to his face that his eyes and his ears and all the passes to his heart were already in the hands of a cruel, ruthless, and masterful enemy? No wonder that you never read the *Holy War*. No wonder that the bulk of men have never once opened it. The *Downfall* is not a favorite book in the night gardens of Paris.

3. And, then, few, very few, it is to be feared, will be any better for the *Holy War*. For, to be any better of such a terrible book as this is, we must at all costs lay it, and lay it all, and lay it all at once, to heart. We must submit ourselves to see ourselves continually in its blazing glass. We must stoop to be told that it is all, in all its terrors and in all its horrors, literally true of ourselves. We must deliberately and resolutely set open every gate that opens in on our heart— Ear-gate and Eye-gate and all the gates of sense and intellect—day and night, to Jesus Christ to enter in; and we must shut and bolt and bar every such gate in the devil's very face, and in the face of all his scouts and orators, day and night also. But who that thinks, and that knows by experience what all that means, will feel himself sufficient for all that? No man. No sinful man. But, among many other noble and blessed things, the *Holy War* will show us that our sufficiency in this impossibility also is all of God. Who, then, will enlist? Who will risk all and enlist? Who

will matriculate in the military school of Mansoul? Who will submit himself to all the severity of its divine discipline? Who will be made willing to throw open and to keep open his whole soul, with all the gates and doors thereof, to all the sieges, assaults, capitulations, submissions, occupations, and such like of the war of gospel holiness? And who will enlist under that banner now?

" 'Set down my name, sir,' said a man of a very stout countenance to him who had the inkhorn at the outer gate. At which those who walked upon the top of the palace broke out in a very pleasant voice,

> "Come in, come in;
> Eternal glory thou shalt win."

We have no longer, after what we have come through, any such stoutness in our countenance, yet will we say tonight with him who had it, Set down my name also, sir!

The Epistles of Paul

And now I began to look into the Bible with new eyes: and, especially, the Epistles of the Apostle Paul were sweet and pleasant to me.

A. W.

THE TRUE DERIVATION of the English word "religion" has long been a disputed question among learned men. But the best scholars of our day are fast coming round to Cicero's root. That great genius in language held that the Latin word *religio* originally meant the continual reading and re-reading of the sacred books. To Tully, as to David, the truly religious man is he whose delight is in the law of the Lord, and in His law doth he meditate day and night. And he shall be like a tree planted by the rivers of water, that bringeth forth his fruit in his season: his leaf also shall not wither; and all that he doeth shall prosper. That is to say, true religion, even in its etymology, stands firm and fruitful in the continual reading of the Word of God, till that Word dwells richly in the assiduous reader's mind and heart. Cicero's etymology continually comes to my mind as often as I open Bunyan's impressive paragraphs on the Bible. And that true etymology comes even more to my mind as often as I open Halyburton's autobiography everywhere. But it is with Bunyan and his new eyes and his new Bible that we have specially to do tonight.

From the beginning to the end of his *Grace Abounding,* Bunyan describes to us the successive eyes with which he read his Bible from first to last. When Bunyan began first to read his Bible it was with the eyes of a child. As a child he greatly delighted in the enthralling stories of the Bible. The garden of Eden, Cain and Abel, Noah and his ark, Abraham and Isaac and Jacob and Joseph, and all their adventures, Moses and his floating cradle among the bulrushes of the Nile, the gigantic labors of Samson, and the pious prowess of David, and so on. Then, through the native strength and the native originality of his mind, though he never went to school to the Fathers or to the early Councils, he began to look into his Bible with the eyes of a student. All our well-read divinity students know those most interesting passages in *Grace Abounding* on the Apocrypha and on the Canon, and such like. And then, after that, the eyes of a sinner intent on seeking his own salvation were given of God to Bunyan. And it is most helpful to ourselves, when we are intent on seeking our own salvation, to see what special parts of the Bible brought salvation to John Bunyan, who writes himself down on his title page as the chief of sinners. And then long afterwards we see him employing his eyes on his Bible as a Puritan preacher. All true preachers are greatly interested in watching what texts Bunyan chose to preach on as he went deeper and deeper into his texts, and as he became more and more spiritual, and more and more evangelical, and more and more experimental, in his preaching. And as we go on through his wonderful book we rejoice to trace how the eyes of a true saint are more and more given him of God, the eyes of his understanding being enlightened that he might know the hope of God's calling, and what the riches of His inheritance in the saints.

After Bunyan had once got his new eyes, this was the way he immediately began to read his Bible and especially his New Testament: "Methought I was as if I had seen Him born; as if I had seen Him grow up; as if I had seen Him walk through this world from His cradle to His cross; to which, also, when He came, I saw how gently He gave Himself to be hanged and nailed upon it, for my sins and wicked doings. Also, as I mused upon this His progress, that scripture dropped upon my spirit, He was ordained for the slaughter." Let us all learn to read our New Testament in that way. For reading in that way is not only a sure evidence to us that we have got new eyes from God, but as we go on to read in that way our eyes will become more and more new every day. Scale after scale will fall from our eyes till we shall see deeper and deeper into the word of God every time we open it. This is what has been called reading with "the eye on the object," which is the only true and fruitful way of reading the Bible and everything else.

"Especially the Epistles of the Apostle Paul were sweet and pleasant to me." If Dr. Thomas Goodwin is right when he says that reconciliation is the main argument of the Bible, then that argument comes to its consummation and its crown in Paul's Epistles. And that was Paul's own conviction and assurance about his Epistles and about his whole apostleship. For he claims in every Epistle of his that to him above all other men had been committed the word of reconciliation. Now, if that is so, then Bunyan is entirely right in his immense indebtedness to Paul. And we also are right if Paul's reconciliation Epistles are immensely sweet and pleasant to us. And in the pulpit they only are the true successors of Paul who say more and more with Paul every new Sabbath day, "Now, then, we are ambassadors for Christ, as though God did beseech you by us: we pray you in Christ's stead, be ye reconciled to God." But you are not preachers of reconciliation like Paul and Bunyan. You are only retired and private readers of Paul's Epistles of reconciliation. Only, are you even that? Have you got your new eyes from God even yet? When you sit down at night for a little heart-sweetening reading after another heart-embittering day to what part of your Bible do you turn your eyes?

Luther said that since he was always sinning so was he always reading *Romans* and *Galatians*. Now, since you are always sinning, what are you always reading? We are all confiding friends here, and I will not ask you such homecoming questions as that without answering for myself. Well, for myself, I often sweeten my heart at the end of the day with this passage out of Paul: "Being justified freely by his grace, through the redemption that is in Christ Jesus, whom God hath set forth to be a propitiation through faith in his blood." Now, if you know anything in all the world more sweet to the sin-embittered heart than that, I would like you to tell me where I can find it. Many of your new eyes have been fastened, like mine, on this also: "To him that worketh not, but believeth on him that justifieth the ungodly, his faith is counted for righteousness." And on this: "Who was delivered for our offences, and was raised again for our justification." And on this: "Where sin abounded, grace did much more abound." And then what consolation and what sweetness there is in the seventh and eighth chapters of Romans, especially when we read those two chapters together at the same down-sitting. Only, do you ever do that? Speak out, and say.

"Indeed, I was then never out of the Bible." Just so. When once any man has really got his new eyes from God, and when once he has fairly gone into his Bible with his new eyes, that man will never again be long out of his Bible. His daily life will not let him be long out of his Bible. And especially his evil heart will not let him be long out of his Bible. His house may be full of books, and not bad books either; but his Bible is the only book of them all that wholly answers to his life around him and especially to his life within him. But let me throw in this parenthetically at this point. Rich and full as John Bunyan is, on the splendid service his Bible did him, our own Halyburton is richer and fuller far. And Jacob Behmen tells an anxious inquirer to cast himself once every hour into the depths of his Bible, aye, every half hour, and he will find himself to be straightway penetrated with the divine glory, and will taste a sweetness that no tongue can express. "Thou wouldst then love thy cross more than all the goods and all the joys of this world." So Jacob Behmen assures his disciple.

"I was then never out of the Bible." Have you ever had a time in your whole life of which you could so speak? When was it? Was it when you first got your new eyes from God? And when it seemed to you as if your new eyes were far too new and far too good for you to throw them away on anything but your Bible? Or was it when some great sin of yours threatened to find you out? Or, again, was it in some great shipwreck of desire and hope when all your other books on which you had fed your desire and your hope had suddenly become so much dust and ashes in your mouth? Was it then that you began to find such a sweetness and such a solace in your Bible that, like Bunyan, you were never out of it? And when, like Jacob Behmen's obedient disciple, you plunged yourself back into your Bible every half hour? A time of a great bereavement also sends some people back in a hurry to their deserted Bible. When their life was full of all manner of prosperity, when their days and nights were full of family affections and family interests, when their head was anointed every day with fresh oil, and when their cup was always running over, in those days they could not away with Paul's Epistles or anything else of that so heavenly kind. But when they sat solitary, and when no man cared for their soul, then their Bible began to come to its own again in their broken hearts. Then, like Bunyan, "it was marvelous to them to find the fitness of God's word to their case. The wonderful rightness of the timing of it, the power, the sweetness, the light, and the glory that all come with it." And then the forsaken soul rose up out of the dust of death, and said, "I will go, and will return to my first Husband, for then it was better with me than now."

"And now I began to look into the Bible with new eyes, and read as I never did before. And, especially, the Epistles of the Apostle Paul were sweet and pleasant to me. And, indeed, I was then never out of the Bible, either by reading or meditation." Delightful! Delightful! But what is this? For I turn the leaf, and I find this: "I am convinced that I am an ignorant sot; and that I want those blessed gifts that other good people have: the blessed gifts of spiritual knowledge and spiritual understanding. For I am tossed continually between the devil and my own ignorance, and am so perplexed, especially at some times, that I cannot tell what to do."

Now, are you not—some of you—secretly glad to hear that? Does that not immensely comfort you? I am sure it does. At any rate, it immensely comforts me. To know that John Bunyan, with all his new eyes and with all his rapturous love for Paul's Epistles, yet at some times felt himself to be a sot of a man, and to be tossed about by the devil and by his own ignorance of divine things—does that not comfort you? At any rate, I say, I for one get great comfort and great hope out of all that, as well as out of such corresponding scriptures as these: "I am dust and ashes," said Abraham; "I am a worm, and no man," said a psalmist; "I am a beast before God," said another psalmist; "I was shapen in iniquity," said the greatest and best of all the psalmists; "I am a man of unclean lips, and all my righteousnesses are but so many filthy rags," said the most evangelical of all the prophets; "I am more brutish than any man," said one of the wisest of men; "I abhor myself," said Job; "I am sold under sin," said Paul; "None but the devil could equal me in pollution of mind and heart," said Bunyan. And, again, "I am an ignorant sot, tossed about by the devil at his will." And so on—in every sincere and genuine saint of God who is undergoing a great sanctification for a great service on earth and in heaven. Dear, sin-tormented people of God, do not be too much cast down. You are in good company. You are in the best of company. Angels envy you and your company. They would exchange all their glory for such an experience and for such a prospect as yours. Meantime, take these sweet and pleasant passages out of Paul, and take them home with you: "There is therefore now no condemnation to them which are in Christ Jesus. And if children, then heirs: heirs of God, and joint-heirs with Christ. If so be that we suffer with him, that we may be also glorified together. And we know that all things work together for good to them that love God. Who shall separate us from the love of Christ? Nay, in all these things we are more than conquerors, through him that loved us. Nor height, nor depth, nor any other creature shall be able to separate us from the love of God, which is in Christ Jesus, our Lord." Wherefore, comfort your hearts with these words, and with a thousand more words like these, in Paul's so sweet and so pleasant Epistles.

Noah

Even after the four full chapters that Moses gives to Noah, Peter, in the New Testament, makes a very important addition to our knowledge of Noah. "Noah the eighth person was a preacher of righteousness," adds the Apostle. We have it in as many words from Moses himself, and he gives almost half of one of his chapters to it, that Noah became a planter of vineyards and an owner of vineyards and a dealer in wine in his old age. But with only eight souls saved, and some of them scarcely saved, there was no evidence at all in Moses that the divine ordinance of preaching had been as yet set up on the earth, and much less that Noah was ordained to that office. Now, as a preacher myself, I have a deep professional interest, as well as some other deep interests, in asking myself why it was that Noah was so signally unsuccessful as a preacher. Was it because it was righteousness that he preached? That may very well have been it; for, so far as my own experience goes, righteousness is the one thing that our hearers will not have at our hands. All other kinds of preaching—polemical preaching, apologetical preaching, historical and biographical preaching, sacramental preaching, evangelical preaching—some of our people will welcome, and, indeed, will demand, but they all will agree in refusing and resenting the preaching of righteousness, the preaching of repentance and reformation, the preaching of conversation and conduct and character. No, they would not have it. Josephus supplements Moses and Second Peter, and tells us that Noah preached and pleaded with them to change their dispositions and their actions, till

137

he was afraid they would kill him. Of one thing we are sure, Noah did not discredit his preaching by his life, as so many of our preachers do. For Noah had this testimony as long as he was a preacher, that he walked with God. "Thee," said the Lord to Noah in giving him his instructions about the ark—"Thee only have I seen righteous before me." My father's tutor, says the author of *The Decline and Fall of the Roman Empire,* believed all that he professed, and practiced all that he enjoined. Could it have been that the preacher's sons and daughters undid all their father's preaching as soon as he had preached it? Physician, heal thyself, did his congregations call out to the preacher of righteousness as he came down from his pulpit and went home to his house? Yes, that would be it. I am almost sure that would be it. For one sinner still destroyeth much good. And we know that Noah had one son—he was his second son, Ham—who helped to bring down his father's gray hairs with sorrow to the grave. What way could a preacher of righteousness be expected to make with a son like his second son among his sons at home? No way at all. It was impossible. That, I feel almost certain, would be it.

I am not to ask you to enter with me into the theophanies of the flood, or into the naval architecture of Noah and Moses, or into the geology that emerged after the flood was over, or into the longevity of Noah and the distribution of his sons. My one and sole aim with you is a practical aim. My one and sole remaining ambition in life is to preach righteousness. To preach righteousness, the nature of it, the means to attain it. To preach righteousness, and all matters connected with righteousness, first to myself, then to my sons, and then to my people. This one thing I do. And in this one light shall I ask you to look at Noah, and at his ark, and at his vineyards, and at his wine, and at Ham, the reprobate son.

Not only did Noah preach his best and his most earnest

as the end drew near; not only Noah himself, but every tree that fell in the forest, and every plank that was laid in the ark, every ax stroke and the echo of every hammer were a louder and ever louder call to the men of that corrupt and violent day to flee from the wrath to come. But, sad to say, the very men without whose help the ark would never have been built, the very men who felled the trees, and planed and laid the planks, and careened and caulked the seams of the finished ship—those very men failed to take passage in that ship for themselves, for their wives and for their children. Many a skilled and high-paid carpenter, many a strong-limbed and grimy-faced blacksmith, and many a finisher and decorator in woodwork and in iron, must have gnashed their teeth and cursed one another when they saw their children drowning all around them, and the ark shut, and borne up, and lifted up above the earth. But those carpenters and blacksmiths and finishers were wise men and their loss was salvation compared with many of those architects and builders and ornamenters of churches who compete with one another and undersell one another in our day. As also compared with all those publishers and printers and booksellers of Bibles, and all those precentors and choirs and organists, and all those elders and deacons and doorkeepers, who are absolutely indispensable to the kingdom of God, but who themselves are all the time outside of it. The Gibeonites in Israel were hewers of wood and drawers of water to Israel; they dwelt in Israel, and had their victuals there, but they were aliens from the commonwealth of Israel. And all Noah's own excellent sermons, all his pulpit appeals about righteousness, and all his crowds of congregations would not have kept his gray head above the rising waters that he had so often described in his sermons had he not himself gone and done what the Lord commanded him to do. That is to say, had he not, only prepared the ark, but also had he not gone into the ark and asked the Lord to shut him in. We ministers may preach the very best of gospels to you, and yet at the end of our ministry be castaways ourselves. "What if I," wrote Rutherford to Lady Kenmure—"What if I, who can have a subscribed testimonial of many who shall stand at the right hand of the Judge, shall myself miss Christ's approval, and be set upon the left hand? There is such a beguile, and it befalleth many. What if it befall me, who have but too much art to cover my own soul and others with the flourish of ministerial, country holiness?" The next Sabbath after that on which Noah preached his last sermon on righteousness sea monsters were already whelpng and stabling in his pulpit.

There had never been such dry seasons since the memory of man. It seemed as if the whole earth would surely die of famine. All the time the ark was a-building the heavens were as brass and the earth as iron. Had Noah preached and prophesied that this terrible drought would last till this generation repented of their corruptions and their violence, there would have been a perfect pentecost among them. Thousands would have turned to the Lord that very day. As it was, many was the day that the worst scoffers at the preachings were of the preacher's own household. Many was the Sabbath day when Noah disappeared into the forest and fell on his face and prayed that he might have a sign from heaven. But still the branches broke into dust and ashes under him as he wrestled with God for even one little cloud in the sky. And all the chapped and blasted earth around him mocked at him and at his sermons and at his threatenings of a flood of water. But all he ever got for answer to his prayer in the woods was what he already knew, and, indeed, every hour of every day called to mind: "My spirit shall not always strive with man. Make thee an ark of gopher wood." Till Noah, moved with fear, returned to his place and worked with all his might for another six days preparing an ark to the saving of his house. The Lord is slow to wrath, slow to a proverb and to a jest. But we have His own warning for it that His spirit will not always strive with man. Not so much as a man's hand of cloud had been seen for weeks and for months in the west. But no sooner was the ark finished and Noah was shut in than God arose and gave the signal. And the stormy wind that fulfills His pleasure struck the ark that moment like a park of artillery. And not the ark only, but the whole creation shook, and shuddered, and groaned, and travailed with the wrath of God. The firmament fell in sunder in the twinkling of an eye, and the waters which were below the firmament leaped up to meet the waters which were above the firmament. And the waters prevailed exceedingly on the earth, and all the high hills that were under the whole heaven were covered. And Noah only remained alive, and they that were with him in the ark.

There has never been anything again on the face of this earth like that ark for the next hundred and fifty days. And there will never be anything like it again till the day of judgment. Such was the wrath of God, and such were the horror and the suspense, the roaring of the storm without, the roaring of the brute beasts within, and the overwhelming fear. There is only one thing that outdoes that ark on this earth, and that is the heart of every regenerate man. No, that is too much to say; not of every regenerate man, but only of that man among the regenerate who has been taken deep down into the noble and saving knowledge of his own heart. With God's judgments against him and against his sin all around him; with his past sin and his present sinfulness finding him out a thousand times every day, knocking at his door, calling in at his window, dogging his steps; with his soul reeling and staggering within him like a drunken man, and with earth and hell let loose within him—that rocking, reeling, midnight ark is a predestinated picture of the soul of every deeply true and deeply exercised saint. Not of sham saints, and not of saints on the surface, but of every son and daughter of fallen Adam who are truly being made in their heart of hearts, and in the divine nature, the sons and daughters of the Lord Almighty, the Lord All-Holy. And most of all are the hearts of God's great saints like that ark in the wild beasts that made that ark hideous to sit in, to eat and drink in, and to sleep and worship in for the next hundred and fifty days and nights. All the evil beasts that ever roared and ravened for their prey were in that ark, each one after his kind. Apes and peacocks were there also, and sparrows and magpies; snakes, and vipers, and adders. Dogs with their vomit and sows with their mire. As the blessed Behmen has it about himself: A man's soul is sometimes like a wolf, sometimes like a dog, sometimes like a lion, sometimes like a serpent—subtle, venomous, and slanderous; sometimes like a toad—poisonous, and so on; till my soul, says that singularly subtle and singularly saintly man, is a cage of cruel and unclean birds. And not Behmen's soul only, but yours and mine, if we really know anything at all about the matter in hand. Those wild beasts are all there till God in His great pity opens the windows of heaven over us and says to us: "O thou afflicted, tossed with tempests, and not comforted. This is as the waters of Noah unto me. The mountains shall depart and the hills be removed, but my kindness shall not depart from thee, neither shall the covenant of my peace be removed, saith the Lord that hath mercy on thee. This is the heritage of the Lord; and their righteousness is of me, saith the Lord."

How did Noah and his household occupy themselves during the whole of that long and dreary voyage? They had no chess and no cards, no old newspapers and no sensational novels. I have no idea how the rest of the family occupied themselves, but I can tell you to a certainty what Noah did. I have no books, said Jacob Behmen, but I have myself. And Noah had himself all those hundred and fifty days and nights. Himself, and Ham, and the woman who had gone down at his door with Ham's name on her drowning lips. He had Shem also, and Japheth, and their wives, and their mother. And if all the romances that ever were written had been on board, and all the games with which men and women have murdered time since time began, do you think that Noah would have had either time or taste for them? What do you think? Do you think he would? There is no way of killing time like prayer. If you would be at the end of your longest voyage before you know where you are, walk with God on the deck of the vessel. Tell Him every day about your children. Tell Him their names. Describe their opening characters to Him. Confide to Him your fears about them. And if one of them has gone astray, or is beginning to go astray, you will have enough in him alone to keep you alone with God for, say, one hour every day. I warrant you the wettest ground under the ark was as dry as tinder before Noah's eyes were dry. They all feared to ask their father why he wept as he walked with God, for they all knew quite well that it was for them that he so walked and so wept.

"And the sons of Noah that went forth of the ark were Shem, Ham, and Japheth." There will be plenty of men that will go forth of earth and into heaven with all Ham's evil memories, and more. But from the north pole to the south pole, and from the rising to the setting of the sun in the new heavens and the new earth there will not be so much as one man found there with Ham's still lewd, still hard, and still impenitent heart.

David—In His Vices

BUTLER HAS A SERMON on self-deceit which you should all read till you have it by heart. If you will listen to him, Butler will prove to you that self-deceit, or internal hypocrisy, is the greatest of all your guilt and the corruption of your whole moral character. He will show you also that David was guilty of this worst of all sins beyond any other saint or sinner in all the Bible. David's is the most prodigious instance of the very wickedest of all the vices of the vicious heart of man. All David's other vices were but skin wounds and surface sores that might soon have been bound up. But David's self-deceit was deep-seated, and it would have been deadly to David but for Nathan, or, rather, but for the Lord. As for David's fall, it was what followed that so displeased the Lord. "It is safer to be wicked in the ordinary way than from this corruption lying at the root." As Thomas Goodwin points out in his treatise on the Aggravation of Sin, it was "the matter of Uriah," even more than the matter of Bathsheba, that awakened the anger of the Lord against David. It was David's sin of deliberation and determination rather than his sin of sudden and intoxicating passion. It was both matters; it was both sins; but it cannot be overlooked that it was after a twelvemonth of self-deceit, internal hypocrisy, and self-forgiving silence on David's part that Nathan was sent to David in such divine indignation. How a man like David could have lived all that time soaked to the eyes in adultery and murder and not go mad is simply inconceivable. That is to say, it would be inconceivable if we had not ourselves out of which to parallel and illustrate David, and thus to make

144

David both possible and natural to us. Before you begin to read and think, as long as you confine your reading and thinking to that of children and fools, you will think it impossible that all the self-deceitfulness and internal hypocrisy that could possibly be in David and in the devil taken together could have so blinded David to the blackness of his sin and to the absolute certainty of God's dreadful judgments. But when you become a man in the books you read, and in the matters of your own heart, you will stop all your childish exclamations over David, and will say to yourself, I myself am David; I myself am that self-deceiving man.

"What the particular circumstances were with which David extenuated his crimes, and quieted and deceived himself, is not related." No. They are not related; but we may guess at some of them to our own self-discovery and self-advantage. David would say to himself such things as these: "I am the king, and Uriah and his wife are both my servants. All that he has is mine. She is not for such as he. She should be a queen, and she shall be. And I can make it up to him, and I will." And then there was Uriah's disobedience and insolence to his king, his open disloyalty and his boasted indifference to his king's discovery and disgrace. "Yes, the sword devoureth one as well as another," David would say. "And it might have devoured Uriah even if I had not written that letter." And then, to repay, and repair, and cover it all up, David fetched the woman to his house, and she became his wife, and bare him a son. And, besides all that, it was all past, and why go back upon the past? David, you may be sure, had all these, and many more than all these, "distinctions to fence with." And then what was wanting in all that himself came in to complete and carry off the case: self, "the most disingenuous and abominable principle that ever was." Self, that utterly ungodly, diabolical, inhuman, inconceivably wicked, and detestable thing that was so strong in David and is so strong in you and in me! He who watches the workings of self in his own mind and heart will not be forward to throw a stone at David; he will not be surprised at anything he reads about David or any other man. He will not wonder either at David's fall or at his subsequent self-deceit. I am warned of God that, with all my study and all my watchfulness and all my prayerfulness, the deceitfulness and the internal hypocrisy of my own heart will still deceive me. Well, all I shall say in answer to that is this, that if my heart is worse than I know it to be, then the God of all grace, with all the blood of His Son, and with all the patience and power of His Spirit, help me! My brethren, beware how you shield yourself from yourself, and use "distinctions" when you are conversing with your conscience about yourself. To be pointed at, and told to his face that he was unclean, and cruel, and cowardly, and guilty of blood, was David's salvation. And to have some one injured enough and angry enough, or friendly and honest and kind enough, to call you to your face false, or cruel, or envious, or all that together, might be the beginning of your salvation. And would he be your enemy who first told you that saving truth? Surely you will not think it. But, far best of all, let my conscience smite me, and about my self-love and my self-deceit in me.

Butler points out at the same time that, portentous as David's internal hypocrisy and self-deceit were, they were all the time local and limited in David. That is to say, his self-deceit had not as yet spread over and corrupted his whole life and character. There was real honesty in David for all this self-deceiving time. David gave scope, in Butler's words, to his affections of compassion and good will, as well as to his passions of another kind. And while this is some comfort to us to hear, there is a great danger to us in this direction also. The whited sepulchers fasted twice in the week, and they gave tithes of all that they possessed. Many of them had begun, like David, with only one thing wrong in their life; but it was a thing that they hushed up in their own consciences, till by that time the self-deceit was spreading and was well-nigh covering with death and damnation their whole life and character. David was rescued from that appalling end; but he was fast on the way to that end when the Lord arrested him. David all the time was administering justice and judgment as boldly, and with as much anger, to evildoers as if there had never been a man of the name of Uriah on the face of the earth. And just because he was making men who had no pity restore the lamb fourfold, just because of that he was more and more confirmed in his own self-deceit. We would need Nathan and his parable at this point. Only, your self-deceit would make you miss his point, till he drove it home into your deceitful heart. You are the man. You are all the more severe with one class of sinners that you sin yourself so much with another and opposite class. You are terrible to see and hear on the sins of the flesh, because you are up to the eyes in the far more fatal sins of the mind. You despise and detest publicans and sinners, while you dine and sup and plot against Christ with Pharisees and internal hypocrites. We all turn away our eyes and our ears from parables like that. Let the man, then, who would discover his own self-deceit, if there is one such, let him turn his eyes in upon his own heart, and especially let him turn his eyes in the opposite direction in his own heart to that in which his easy and untempted virtue displays itself.

But so bold, and towering, and self-deceived is our self-deceit, that it invades and entrenches itself, not in the matters of morals only; it comes to its fullness and to a positive grandeur in our devotions, in our daily dealings with God Himself. Nothing can be more open and notorious than the self-deceit and utter hypocrisy of our psalms and our prayers. David says, and no doubt from his own devotional experience, that if he regards iniquity in his heart, the Lord will not hear him. How much less would the Lord have heard him if he had carried out his iniquity openly, and had put all the deepest deceit of his heart into his psalms and prayers, as we do. I do not read that David composed any penitential psalms during those self-deceiving months. And yet there is no saying. There is no limit to the sacrilege and profanity of an internal hypocrisy. Be that as it may, if David did not, we do. What could be more deceitful than our public worship? Stop and think over the next psalm that is given out, and say if you have forehead enough to sing it after you understand it. And, whether you do that or no, let any man venture with a counsel, or a correction, or a warning, or a reproof, and he will not take you at your word in the church or in the prayer-meeting again. Woe to the man who believes that you are in earnest as you prostrate yourself before God and man in your psalms and prayers. You will soon undeceive him if he thinks that you are broken and contrite in heart, or meek and lowly in heart, or that you lack wisdom, love the cross, wait for light, and are the little children of the kingdom of heaven.

He was a happy preacher whose pulpit awakened David and brought David back to God. Nathan took his life in his hand that day. But he had his reward. And what a reward it was! Think of having David's soul set down to your account at the great day! What shall we ourselves owe to Nathan at that day for that sermon? We would never have had David's psalms but for Nathan's sermon. And what should we have done, I cannot conceive, without David's psalms. Preaching is magnificent work if only we could get preachers like Nathan. If our preachers had only something of Nathan's courage, skill, serpent-like wisdom, and evangelical instancy! But even Nathan himself would be helpless with some of you. You would have turned upon Nathan; you would have taken his good name and his life; you would have written a letter about him to Joab at Rabbah. Brutus never read a book but to make himself a better man. When will that be said about your coming to church? Happy the preacher who has so much as one Brutus a Sabbath day among his hearers! Happy the preacher who has a David among his hearers from time to time, so that he can pass on and say to him, The Lord also hath put away thy sin! We ministers must far more study Nathan's method, especially when we are sent to preach awakening sermons. Too much skill cannot be expended in laying down our approaches to the consciences of our people. Nathan's sword was within an inch of David's conscience before David knew that Nathan had a sword. One sudden thrust, and the king was at Nathan's feet. What a rebuke of our slovenly, unskilful, blundering work! When we go back to Nathan and David, we forget and forgive everything that had been evil in David. The only thing wanting to make that day in David's life perfect was that Nathan should have had to come to David.

Now, what will make this the most perfect day in all your life will be this, if you will save the Lord and His prophet all that trouble, and be both the Lord and His prophet to yourself. Read Nathan's parable to yourself till you say, I am the man! And so ever after with every parable, and with every psalm, and with every prayer, and with everything of that kind. When we preach anything of that kind, all the time we are preaching, be you fast kindling your own anger against yourself. And as soon as we are done preaching, speak you out in yourself and at yourself, and say, As the Lord liveth, the man that hath done this thing shall surely die. And, always, when the Thirty-second Psalm is announced to be sung, and when innocent men and women and children are getting their instruments of music ready, be you getting yourself ready, till you cannot wait for them. Blessed is the man! —lead the congregation, and sing. And, when, by a happy inspiration the Fifty-first Psalm is again given out, do you ejaculate that there is such a psalm in existence. For it is new to you every morning and every night. "I conceal nothing," sobbed Bishop Lancelot Andrewes every Lord's Day morning before he could face his congregation and his clergy. "I make no excuses. I denounce against myself my sins. Indeed, I have sinned against the Lord, and thus and thus have I done. O Lord, I have destroyed myself. Say, O God, unto my soul, I am thy salvation!"

And, then, David's "way of lying." Did any of you ever suppress and keep silent about your principles, say, at an election time? Did you ever hedge and double in your public life in order to get a post, or in order to stand well with those who have posts and pieces of bread to give away? Did you ever tune a speech or a sermon or a prayer to turn away the anger of a man whose anger you feared, or with an eye to a man you wished to stand well with? Or did you ever "tell a vain lie upon yourself," ascribing something falsely or exaggeratingly to yourself through vanity or other self-interest? And, alongside of that, when and where did you last forward, or allow another to put forward, a detracting word about your friend or about your rival, and hold back what you felt would be for his advantage? Then the story of David and the priest of Nob is, in that case, written for your learning. You will see in that chapter how David obtained hallowed bread of Ahimelech, and what that bread cost Ahimelech and his house. "Remove from me the way of lying, and grant me Thy law graciously. He points to the sore of his guileful heart," says Thomas Goodwin, "wherein his grief lay. David, among other corruptions, had a lying spirit sometimes."

Or, again, were you ever driven to simulate sickness, or even madness, in order to get out of some dreadful crime or scrape you had fallen into? See, then, God's compassion for you, at David's cost, in His having had that so humiliating chapter put into your Bible. What a state of mind must David have been in that day when the servants of King Achish led David like a madman or a wild beast to the borders of their land, and then let him loose as you would let

loose and hound out a madman or a wild beast you were
terrified at! O what a bottomless mystery and misery and
agony of sin and shame the heart of man is, and, most of all,
the heart of a man after God's own heart! From the same
fountain will spring forth, on sufficient temptation and opportunity, the noblest deeds, and the most debasing and
despicable. Had it not been in the Bible, we would have denounced that chapter as the cruelest, the most blasphemous,
and the most utterly impossible slander. And, then, to have
two splendid psalms as the immediate outcome of that sickening chapter! Truly they would need to be men in understanding, and not children, who read the Bible. For,

> Not in their brightness, but their earthly stains,
> Are the true seed vouchsafed to earthly eyes,
> And saints are lowered that the world may rise.

Stephen

In the stoning of Stephen there was lost to the Pentecostal Church another Apostle Paul. Stephen was a young man of such original genius and of such special grace that there was nothing he might not have attained to had he been allowed to live. His wonderful openness of mind; his perfect freedom from all the prepossessions, prejudices, and superstitions of his day; his courage, his eloquence, his spotless character, with a certain sweet, and at the same time majestic, manner, all combined to set Stephen in the very front rank both of service and of risk. In all these things, and especially in the openness, receptiveness, and ripeness of his mind, Stephen far outstripped even such pillar apostles as Peter and James and John themselves. Stephen had anticipated also, and had forerun, and had all but carried off, the apostolic palm from Paul himself. All these things made Stephen already all but the foremost man of his day, and, as a consequence, the first man to be struck at and struck down. Simple deacon and servant of tables as Stephen was, it was impossible that a man of such ability and such distinction should be confined and limited to that. His intellectual power, his spiritual insight and foresight, with the strength of his faith and the warmth of his devotion, were all such that he soon found himself deep in apostolic duty, as well as in the proper work of the deaconship. After his purely deaconship work was done, and springing immediately out of his way of doing it, Stephen felt himself constrained on many occasions to take a still more public part in the support and the defense and the dedication of the infant Church of Jerusalem. But malice always follows eminence in this world, as Stephen soon found out to his cost. Ignorance, superstition, prejudice, ill-will, odium, all began to dog Stephen's footsteps and to raise their murderous misrepresentations against him in every synagogue into which he entered. And the better he spoke, and the more unanswerably, the more were the enemies that he raised both against himself and against the truth, till his enemies had their own way with him. "We have heard him speak blasphemous words against Moses, and against God." That was his indictment, as we say; and then we have his apology in the seventh chapter of the Acts, and a very remarkable piece of speaking it is in many ways.

As often as we hear of an Apology we always think of Socrates. On the other hand, our Lord, when on His trial, offered no Apology. He held His peace, insomuch that the governor marveled greatly. What, I reverently wonder, would His Apology have been? You who are students of the New Testament might do worse, now that your college exercises are nearly over, than to continue your great studies and try to construct, with all your learning and ability and insight, the Apology that our Lord, had He seen fit, might have addressed to that same Council. An intelligent congregation would greatly delight in that supposed Apology for a Sabbath evening lecture if you did it well. At any rate, if your sense of reverence will not let you put His Apology into your Master's mouth, you might do this: you might some time take the trouble to compare the Apology that Plato puts into his Master's mouth with this Apology of Stephen that you have here in Luke. The one, the first great defense of truth and righteousness in the Pagan Dispensation; and the other, the first great defense of Christ and His infant Church in the Apostolic and Evangelic Dispensation. "Men, brethren, and fathers, hearken!" Stephen commences. Always commence by conciliating your audience, says Dante. In his introduction, says Augustine, Stephen practices the Quintilian art of capturing the good will of his hearers, however stoutly and sternly and plain-spokenly he may have to end.

It almost looks as if we had Stephen's Apology verbatim in the Book of the Acts. His speech reads as well to us as if we had sat in the Council that day and had heard it with our own ears. The beloved physician, when he turned church historian, had a perfect understanding of all things from the very first; and, among other things, he supplies us with remarkably full reports of some of the great sermons and speeches and apologies of that all-important time. Sometimes a single word, sometimes an accent on a single word, sometimes the shaping and insertion of a single phrase, sometimes a quotation or a paraphrase of a quotation, sometimes what he does not say, as well as what he does say; sometimes what he manages to suggest without saying it at all—little things like these will discover and proclaim the true orator. And that is the case again and again in Stephen's Apology. Pericles, Plutarch tells us, never spoke that he did not leave a secret sting in the hearts of his hearers. And all Stephen's eloquent review of Old Testament history drew on and gathered itself up to drive this terrible sting through and through the hearts of the whole Council, "As your fathers did, so do ye! For ye have now been the betrayers and murderers of the Just One!"

Now, out of all that, quite a crowd of lessons and instructions and examples and warnings rise up before us, and press themselves upon us. Let us select two or three of those lessons and for the present leave the others unspoken.

1. Up to this time the twelve had done everything with their own hands. They had been evangelists, preachers, apologists, pastors, ruling elders, session clerks, servants of tables, and everything else, for the daily increasing congregations of Jerusalem and the whole country round about.

But it was the money matters of the Pentecostal Church that completely broke the apostles down and brought things to a perfect standstill. When thousands of people were contributing to a central sustentation fund, and were again, rich and poor, supported out of it; when the rich were selling their possessions and were laying the prices at the apostles' feet; and when the increasing crowds of poor members were receiving their daily dole directly from the apostles' hands, it is plain that all this would soon result in the serious encroachment of the secular side of their work, so to call it, on the purely spiritual side. Their public teaching and preaching, and certain still more important matters, would be seriously interfered with, till the twelve apostles took the wise step that is recorded in this chapter. It is not reason, they said, and we cannot go on with it, that we should leave the Word of God in order to serve tables to this extent. Wherefore, brethren, look out among yourselves seven men whom we may appoint over this business. And we will, all the more, give ourselves continually to prayer and to the ministry of the Word. And this proposal of the apostles commended itself to the common sense of the whole Church, and they chose seven select men and set them before the apostles for ordination. And we inherit the wisdom and the benefit of that apostolic example to this day.

The Church of our day also says to her members and to her office-bearers something like this: "It is utterly unreasonable that our ministers should all alone be expected to perform all the multitudinous work that arises out of a great congregation. It is quite preposterous that any one man should be expected to preach two or three sermons a week, keep in close contact with a thousand people, baptize our children, marry our sons and daughters, console our sick, bury our dead, find work for our unemployed, negotiate loans of money and gather gifts for our embarrassed members, get our aged and our orphaned into asylums and hospitals, besides many other things that can neither be foreseen nor set aside by our ministers." And thus it comes about that a compact is entered into and a division of labor is made. The young men take the financing of the congregation off their minister's hands, while the more experienced men share with him in the teaching and the ruling and the visiting of the flock. Never more than just at the present day did the Church see the divine wisdom of the apostolic institution of the deaconship, or feel more the need of adhering to it and extending it. And then the minister who honestly performs his part of the compact in prayer and in preaching will not lack, any more than Peter and John lacked, the willing and capable help of Stephen and Philip. As James Durham says: "In all this we see what a minister's great task is, and wherein he should be taken up—secret prayer, reading, and meditation, and then the public preaching of the Gospel. We see also that though all ministers are virtually both elders and deacons as the twelve were, yet ought they to regulate both of these offices with respect to the former two of secret prayer and public preaching. As also that elders and deacons ought to have respect to keep ministers from being overburdened and too much toiled, that they may have freedom to follow their main work. Yea, even to have frequent and lengthened access to aloneness and solitariness, which is both most necessary as well as well becoming in a minister." And so on at great depth and fullness in "The Dying Man's Testimony to the Church of Scotland."

2. *Nomina debita,* says John Donne; that is to say, "Every man owes to the world the signification of his name, and of all his name. Every new addition of honor or of office lays a new obligation upon him, and his Christian name above all." Now, when you name a man a deacon, as the apostles named Stephen, from the day you do so he begins to owe to

the world and to the Church some new obligations. He is called and ordained and named because he is a man of honest report, and full of wisdom and devotedness; and all these graces grow in every new deacon as he goes on to exercise them. I do not know so well how it is with other Deacons' Courts, but I know to my continual delight and refreshment how it is with our own. I know how nobly our deacons fulfill the Pentecostal program. And that is why our name as a congregation stands in such honor among the congregations of the land. It is our deacons who do it. It is the successors of Stephen and Philip who do it. Every penny of our Pentecostal thousands is collected personally by our deacons. And collected, too, with a spontaneity and a punctuality and a knowledge of what they are doing, and a love for what they are doing, that make our monthly meetings one of the greatest delights and refreshments of my whole ministerial life. It all depends on our clerk, and on our treasurer, and on our censor, and on our splendid staff; all our ability to serve the tables of our poorer brethren depends absolutely on our deacons. Take away our deacons, or let them stand idle while other people do their work, and we would very soon drop down from the front rank to which they and they alone have raised us. "Bring ye all the tithes into the storehouse, that there may be meat in mine house, and prove me now herewith, saith the Lord of hosts, if I will not open you the windows of heaven, and pour you out a blessing, that there shall not be room enough to receive it." It is because our Stephen-like staff hear their Master saying that to them every month that they purchase to themselves such a good degree, they purchase for Free St. George's congregation such a good degree also. Wherefore, all my brethren, look ye out among you men of mind, and men of heart, and men of business habits, and they will purchase a good degree for you also when you appoint them over this business. I wish only that every deacon in Scotland could come and see how our deacons in Edinburgh do their work.

3. And now to pass on to the day when Stephen finished his course, kept the faith, and resigned the deaconship. "Behold," he exclaimed with the stones crashing about his head, "I see the Son of man standing on the right hand of God." But the Son of man does not now any more stand, surely. For when He had by Himself purged our sins He surely sat down forever on the right hand of God. "Sit, said the Lord to my Lord, at my right hand until I make thy foes thy footstool." But, with all that, He could not sit still when He saw them stoning Stephen. And so it is with Him always. He sits, or He stands, or He comes down to earth again, just according to our need, and just according to our faith. I see Him standing up, says Stephen. What a power, what a possession, is faith! For faith can make the Son of man do almost anything she likes. As William Guthrie says of her, "Faith sometimes acts in a very wilful way upon her Lord." So she does. For look at what a willful way the Syrophœnician woman acted on her Lord, till, to get rid of her, He said to her, Take anything you like. Only go home to your daughter. And so still. The faith of His people gives Him absolutely no rest. Their faith makes Him stand up long after He has sat down. Their faith makes Him do everything and be everything that they need and ask. He did everything on earth, and He still does everything in heaven, by which He can be useful to poor souls. As, for example, is the soul naked? Then Christ on the spot is fine raiment. Is the soul hungry and thirsty? Immediately Christ is its milk and its wine, its bread of life and its true manna. Is the avenger of blood at the heels of the sinner? Then just one step and the blood-guilty man is in the city of refuge. In one word, tell Him how He can help a poor sinner who has no other help, and all the high and honorable seats in heaven will not hold our Lord down. And

then, as He honors faith, so faith honors Him. Is He a bridegroom? Faith is in His arms. Is He a shepherd? Faith is at His feet. Is He a rock? Faith has already begun to build her house on Him for eternity. Is He the way? Faith runs with all her affections to the Father by Him. "And they stoned Stephen, calling upon God, and saying, Behold, I see the Son of man standing on the right hand of God. Lord Jesus, receive my spirit. And he kneeled down, and cried with a loud voice, Lord, lay not this sin to their charge. And when he had said this, he fell asleep." For they that have used the office of a deacon well purchase to themselves a good degree, and great boldness in the faith which is in Christ Jesus.

The Angel of the Church at Ephesus

You are not to think of an angel with six wings. This is neither a Michael nor a Gabriel. I cannot give you this man's name, but you may safely take it that he was simply one of the oldest of the office-bearers of Ephesus. No, he was no angel. He was just a chosen and faithful elder who had begun by being a deacon and who had purchased to himself a good degree, like any one of yourselves. Only, by reason of his great age and his spotless character and his outstanding services, he had by this time risen till he was now at the head of what we would call the kirk session of Ephesus. By universal acclamation he was now the "president of their company, and the moderator of their actions," as Dr. John Rainoldes has it. This angel, so to call him, had grown gray in his eldership and he was beginning to feel that the day could not now be very far distant when he would be able to lay down his office forever. At the same time, it looked to him but like yesterday when he had heard the prince of the apostles saying to him those never-to-be-forgotten words, "Take heed to thyself, and to all the flock over which the Holy Ghost hath made thee an overseer, to feed the flock of God, which he hath purchased with his own blood." And, with many mistakes, and with many shortcomings, this ruling and teaching elder of Ephesus has not been wholly unmindful of his ordination vows. In short, this so-called angel of the Church of Ephesus was no more an actual angel than I am. A real angel is an angel. And we cannot attain to a real angel's nature, or to his office, so as to describe such an angel aright. But we understand this Ephesus elder's nature and office quite well. We see his very same office every day among ourselves. For his office was just to feed the flock of God, as Paul has it. And again, as James has it, his office was just to visit the widows and orphans of Ephesus in their affliction, and to keep himself unspotted from the world of Ephesus. And he who has been elected of God to such an office as that in Ephesus, or in Edinburgh, or anywhere else, has no need to envy the most shining angel in all the seven heavens. For the most far-shining angel in the seventh heaven itself desires to look down into the pulpit and the pastorate of the humblest and obscurest minister in the Church of Christ. And that because he knows quite well that there is nothing for him to do in the whole of heaven for one moment to be compared with the daily round on this earth of a minister, or an elder, or a deacon, or a collector, or a Sabbath-school teacher.

Now, there is nothing so sweet, either among angels or among men, as to be appreciated and praised. To be appreciated and praised is the wine that maketh glad the heart of God and man. And the heart of the old minister of Ephesus was made so glad when he began to read this Epistle that he almost died with delight. And then as His all-seeing and all-rewarding way always is, His Lord descended to instances and particulars in His appreciation and praise of His servant. "I know thy works. I chose thee. I gave thee all thy talents. I elected thee to thy charge in Ephesus. I ordained thee to that charge, and my right hand hath held thee up in it. Thou hast never been out of my mind or out of my eye or out of my hand for a moment. I have seen all thy work as thou wentest about doing it for me. It is all written before me in my book. All thy tears also are in my bottle."

We have an old-fashioned English word that exactly sets

forth what our Lord says next to the angel of Ephesus. "I know all thy painfulness also," He says. It is a most excellent expression for our Master's purpose. No other language has produced so many painful ministers as the English language, and no other language can so well describe them. For just what does this painfulness mean? It means all that is left behind for us to fill up of His own painful sufferings. It means all that tribulation through which every true minister of His goes up. It means cutting off now a right hand and plucking out now a right eye. It means taking up some ministerial cross every day. It means drinking every day the cup of the sinfulness of sin. It means to me old Thomas Shepard more than any other minister that I know. "Labor," as our bloodless version has it, is a far too dry, a far too wooden, and a far too tearless, word for our Lord to employ toward such servants of His. Depend on it, He will not content Himself with saying "labor" only. He will select and will distinguish His words on that day. And to all who among ourselves have preached and prayed and have examined themselves in and after their preaching and praying, as it would seem that this angel at one time did, and as Thomas Shepard always did, their Master will signalize and appreciate and praise their "painfulness" in their own so expressive old English, and they will appreciate and appropriate His so suitable word and will appreciate and praise Him back again for it.

His patience is another of the praises that his Master gives to this once happy minister. I do not suppose that the angel of Ephesus counted himself a specially happy man when, all unthought of to himself, he was laying up in heaven all this eulogium on himself and on his patience. But all the more, with such a suffering servant, his Master held Himself bound to take special knowledge of all that went on in the Church of Ephesus. And to this day, and among all our so altered circumstances, patience continues to take a foremost place in the heart and in all the ministry of every successor of the true apostleship. Nay, patience was not only an apostolic grace, it was much more a Messianic grace. Patience was one of the most outstanding and far-shining graces of our Lord Himself as long as He was by far the most sorely tried of all His Father's ministers. And He has all men and all things in His hands to this day that He may so order all men and all things as that all His ministers shall be put to this school all their days, as He was put all His days by His Father. The whole of every minister's lot and life is divinely ordained him so as to win for him his crown of patience, if only he will listen and believe it. "I know all thy patience," said our Lord to the angel of Ephesus.

I do not the least know who or what the Nicolaitanes of Ephesus were, and no one that I have consulted is any wiser than I am, unless it is Pascal. And Pascal says that their name is equivocal. When that great genius and great saint comes on the Nicolaitanes in these Epistles, he has an original way of interpretation all his own. He always interprets this name, so he tells us, of his own bad passions. And not the Nicolaitanes of Ephesus only, but the Egyptians, and the Babylonians, and as often as the name of any "enemy" occurs in the Old Testament, and it occurs in the psalms continually, that so great and so original man interprets and translates them all into his own sinful thoughts and sinful feelings and sinful words and sinful actions. That is, I fear, a far too mystical and equivocal interpretation for most of us as yet. To call the Nicolaitanes of Ephesus our own wicked hearts is far too Port-Royal and puritan for such literalists as we are. Only, as one can see, the minister of Ephesus would be swept into the deepest places, and into the most spiritual experiences, both of mysticism and of puritanism, before their time, as often as he set himself, as he must surely have henceforth set himself every day of his life, to hate the deeds of the Nicolaitanes, whoever they were, and at the same time to love the Nicolaitanes themselves. To a neighbor minister in the same Synod our Lord sends a special message about the sharp sword with the two edges. And it would need all the sharpness of that sword and all its edges to divide asunder the deeds of the Nicolaitanes from the Nicolaitanes themselves in their minister's heart, to divide them, that is, so as to hate their evil deeds with a perfect hatred, and at the same time to love the doers of those deeds with a perfect love. The name "Nicolaitane" is equivocal, says Pascal.

A *litotes* is a rhetorical device by means of which far less is said than is intended to be understood. A true *litotes* has this intention and this result, that while, in words, it diminishes what is actually said, in reality, it greatly increases the effect of what is said. What could be a more condemning charge against any minister of Christ than to tell him in plain words that he had left his first love to his Master and to his Master's work? And yet, just by the peculiar way in which that charge is here worded, a far more sudden blow is dealt to this minister's heart than if the charge had been made in the plainest and sternest terms. To say, "Nevertheless I have somewhat against thee"—to say "somewhat," as if it were some very small matter, and scarcely worth mentioning, and then suddenly to say what it is, that, you may depend on it, gave a shock of horror to that minister's heart that he did not soon get over. You would have thought such a minister impossible. Had you heard his praise so generously spread abroad at first by both God and man you would have felt absolutely sure of that minister's spiritual prosperity and praise to the very end. You would have felt as sure as sure could be that behind all that so immense activity and popularity there must lie hidden a heart as full as it could hold of the deepest and solidest peace with God, a peace, you would have felt sure, without a speck on it, and with no controversy on Christ's part within a thousand miles of it. But the ministerial heart is deceitful above all other men's hearts. And these shocking revelations about this much-lauded minister have been recorded and preserved in order that all ministers may see themselves in them as in a glass. Now, there is not one moment's doubt about when and where all this terrible declension and decay began to set in. His Master does not say in so many words just when and where matters began to go wrong between the two. But that silence of His is just another of His rhetorical devices. He does not tell it from the housetops of Ephesus as yet. But the minister of Ephesus knew quite well, both when and where his first love began to fail and he to fall away. He knew quite well, without his Master's message about it, that all this declension and collapse began in the time and at the place of secret prayer. For, not this Ephesus minister only, but every minister everywhere continues to love his Master and his Master's work, aye, and his Master's enemies, exactly in the measure of his secret reading of Holy Scripture and his secret prayerfulness.

Yes, without being told it in so many words, I am as sure of it as if I had been that metropolitan minister myself. You may depend on it, nay, you know it yourselves quite well, that it was his habitual and long-continued neglect of secret prayer. It was from that declension and decay that his ministry became so undermined and now had come so near a great catastrophe. "With all my past praise of thee, I give thee this warning," said that Voice which is as the sound of many waters, "that unless thou returnest to thy first life of closet communion with me, I will come to thee quickly and will remove thy candlestick out of its place. I gave thee that congregation when I might have given it to another. And I have upheld thee in it, and have delivered thee out of a thousand distresses of thine. But thou hast wearied of me. Thou hast given thy night watches to other things than a true minister's meditation and prayer for himself and for his people. And I will suffer it at thy hands no longer. Remember from whence thou hast fallen, and repent, and do the first works."

And now with all that in closing take this as the secret prayer of the angel of Ephesus the very first night after this severe message was delivered to him. "O thou that holdest the stars in thy right hand, and walkest in the midst of the seven golden candlesticks, thou hast spoken in thy mercy to me. And thou hast given me an ear to hear thy merciful words toward me. Lord, I repent. At thy call I repent. I repent of many things in my ministry in Ephesus. But of nothing so much as of my restraint of secret prayer. This has been my besetting sin. This has been the worm at the root of all my mistakes and misfortunes in my ministry. This has been my blame. O spare me according to thy word. O suffer me a little longer that I may yet serve thee. What profit is there in my blood? Shall the dead hold communion with thee? Shall the grave of a castaway minister redound honour to thee? Restore thou my soul. Restore once more to me the joy of thy salvation, then will I teach transgressors thy ways, and sinners shall be converted to thee. The sacrifices of God are a broken spirit; a broken and a contrite heart, O God, thou wilt not despise. Do good in thy good pleasure unto Zion; build thou the walls of Jerusalem."

Paul as the Chief of Sinners

Everybody knows what the most eminent saints of Holy Scripture think and say of their sinfulness. And here is what some of the most eminent saints who have lived since the days of Holy Scripture have felt and said about their own exceeding sinfulness also. And to begin with, one of the very saintliest of them all—Samuel Rutherford. "When I look at my sinfulness," says Rutherford, "my salvation is to me my Saviour's greatest miracle. He has done nothing in heaven or on earth like my salvation." And the title page of John Bunyan's incomparable autobiography runs thus: "Grace abounding to John Bunyan, the chief of sinners. Come and hear, all ye that fear God, and I will declare what He hath done for my soul." "Is there but one spider in all this room?" asked the Interpreter. Then the water stood in Christiana's eyes, for she was a woman quick of apprehension, and she said, "Yes, Lord, there is more here than one: yea, and spiders whose venom is far more destructive than that which is in her." "My daughters," said Santa Teresa on her deathbed, "do not follow my example; for I have been the most sinful woman in all the world." But what she most dwelt on as she died was that half verse, "*Cor contritum*—a broken and contrite heart, O God, thou wilt not despise." "Do not mistake me," said Jacob Behmen, "for my heart is as full as it can hold of all malice at you and all ill-will. My heart is the very dunghill of the devil, and it is no easy work to wrestle with him on his own chosen ground. But wrestle with him on that ground of his I must, and that the whole of my life to the end." "Begone, all ye self-ignorant and false flatterers!" shouted Philip Neri at them. "I am good for nothing but to do evil." "When a man like me," says Luther, "comes to know the plague of his own heart, he is not miserable only—he is absolute misery itself; he is not sinful only—he is absolute sin itself." "I am made of sin," sobbed Bishop Andrewes, till his private prayer book was all but unreadable to his heirs because of its author's sweat and tears. "It has often appeared to me," says Jonathan Edwards, "that if God were to mark my heart iniquity my bed would be in hell." "I sat down on the side of a stank," [1] says Lord Brodie, "and was disgusted at the toads and esks[2] and many other unclean creatures I saw sweltering there. But all the time my own heart was far worse earth to me, and filthier far than the filthy earth I sat upon." "This is a faithful saying," says Paul, "and worthy of all acceptation, that Christ Jesus came into the world to save sinners, of whom I am chief." Well may our Saviour stop us and ask us whether or no we have counted the cost of being one of His out-and-out disciples!

I can very well believe that there are some new beginners here who are terribly staggered with all that. They were brought up positively to worship the Apostle Paul, and Luther, and Rutherford, and Bunyan. And how such saints of God can write such bitter things against themselves you cannot understand. You would like to acquiesce in all that these men say about all such matters as sin and sinfulness; but you do not see how they can honestly and truly say such things as the above about themselves.

> Fool! said my muse to me,
> Look in thy heart and write.

Remember these two lines of the true poet. Though they were not written about sin, they never come to their fullest

[1] ditch.   [2] newts.

truth and their most fruitful application till they are taken home by the sinner who is seeking sanctification. Yes, look well into your own heart and you will find there the true explanation of your perplexity about Paul, and Luther, and Rutherford, and Bunyan, and all the rest. For your own heart holds the secret to you of this whole matter. If you have any real knowledge of your own heart at all, this cannot possibly have escaped you, that there are things in your own heart that are most shocking and prostrating for you to find there. There are thoughts in your heart, and feelings, and wishes, and likes and dislikes; things you have to hide, and things you cannot hide—things that if you have any religion at all you must take on your knees to Jesus Christ every day, and things you cannot take even to Him short of His sin-atoning blood. Well, you have in all that the true key to Paul's heart, and to the hearts of all the rest. So much so that if you advance as you have begun you also will soon be staggering new beginners yourselves with the scriptures you read, and with the psalms and hymns you select, and with the petitions you offer ere ever you are aware; and, it may yet be, with the autobiography you will yet write to tell to all that fear God what He hath done for your soul. Just go on in the lessons of that inward school, and you will soon stagger us all by passion that you, as well as David and Asaph, will put into the most penitential of psalms.

"The highest flames are the most tremulous," says Jeremy Taylor. That is to say, the holiest men are the most full of holy fear, holy penitence, holy humility, and holy love. And all that is so because the more true spirituality of mind any man has, the more exquisite will be that man's sensibility to sin and to the exceeding sinfulness of sin. "The saints of God are far too sharp-sighted for their own self-satisfaction," says William Guthrie in his golden little book. So they are. For by so much the holier men they become in the sight and estimation both of God and man, the more hideous and the more hopeless do they become to themselves. Such is their more and more sharpened insight into their own remaining sinfulness. Even when God is on the point of translating them to Himself because they so please Him, at that very moment they feel that they were never so near being absolute castaways. When all other men are worshiping them for their saintliness, and rightly so, those right saints of God are gnashing their teeth at the deviltries that are still rampant in their own heart. They hate themselves the more you love them. They curse themselves the more you bless them. The more you exalt and enthrone them, the more they lie with their faces on the earth. When you load them with honors, and banquet them with praises, they make ashes their bread and tears their drink. Their whole head will be waters, and their eyes one fountain of tears just at that moment when God is rising up in compassion, and in recompense, to wipe all tears from their eyes forever.

And it is the sight of God that does it. It is the sight of Jesus Christ that does it. It is God's holy law of love entering our hearts ever deeper and deeper that does it. It is when I take my own heart, with all its wickedness-working self-love, and with all its self-seeking in everything, and self-serving out of everything and every one; with all its deceitfulness, and disingenuousness, and envy, and jealousy, and grudging, and malevolence, and lay it alongside of the holy heart of my Lord—it is that that does it. It is then that I sit down at a stank side with poor Lord Brodie. It is then that my midnight Bible begins to open at unwonted places, and I begin to make bosom friends of unwonted people. It is then that I search the Book of Job, say, not any more for its incomparable dialectic and its noble literature. All these things, as Halyburton has it, have now become comparatively distasteful, then without taste and insipid, as Job himself says about the white of an egg. No, my soul turns in its agony of pain and shame and seeks an utterance for itself in such consummating passages as these. "I have heard of thee by the hearing of the ear: but now mine eye seeth thee. Wherefore I abhor myself, and repent in dust and ashes. Behold, I am vile: what shall I answer thee? I will lay my hand upon my mouth." And from that my Bible begins to open at the right places for me in David, and in Asaph, and in Ezra, and in Daniel, and in Peter, and in Paul, and so on to all Paul-like men down to my own day. And thus it comes about that the authors who are classical to me now are not the ephemerides[1] in religion or in literature that I used to waste my time and my money on when I was a neophyte. My true classics now are those masterly men who look into their own hearts and then write for my heart. It is the sight of God that has made them the writers they are, and it is the same sight that is at last making me the reader that I, too late, am beginning to be. It is the sight of God that does it, till my sinfulness takes such a deep spiritualness, and such a high exclusiveness, and such a hidden secretness, that I can find fit utterance for all that is within me in David, and in David's greatest psalms alone. As thus: "Against thee, thee only, have I sinned, and done this evil in thy sight. The sacrifices of God are a broken spirit: Create in me a clean heart, O God; and renew a right spirit within me."

It was their own sin, or, to speak much more exactly, it was their own sinfulness, that so humbled Rutherford and Bunyan and Christiana and Teresa, and broke their hearts. Nothing at all humiliates, nothing really touches the hearts of people like them but the inward sinfulness of their own hearts. We shallow-hearted fools would think and would say that it was some great crime or open scandal that those saintly men and women had fallen into. Oh, no! There were no men or women in their day of so blameless a name

[1] Publications of transient interest.

as they. One of themselves used to say that it was not "so humiliating and heart-breaking to be sometimes like a beast, as to be always like a devil. But to be both!" he cried out in his twofold agony. The things of this world also that so humiliate all other men do not any more bring so much as a momentary blush to men like Rutherford and women like Teresa. Just go over the things that humiliate and shame you in your earthly life and its circumstances, and then pass over into the ranks of God's saints, and you will there enter on a career of humiliation that will quite drink up the things that make you so shamed now, till you will completely forget their very existence. What I am at this moment contending for is this, that sin alone truly humiliates a saint, even as holiness alone truly exalts him. It was sin, and especially sinfulness, that made those great saints cry out as they did.

A Greek fortuneteller once was reading Socrates' hands and face to discern his true character and to advertise to the people of Athens of his real deserts. And as he went on he startled the whole assembly by pronouncing Socrates to be the most incontinent and libidinous man in all the city, the greatest extortioner and thief, and even worse things than all that. And when the enraged crowd were about to fall on the soothsayer and tear him to pieces for saying such things about their greatest saint, Socrates himself came forward and restrained their anger and confessed openly and said, "Ye men of Athens, let this truth-speaking man alone, and do him no harm. He has said nothing amiss about me. For there is no man among you all who is by nature more predisposed to all these evil things than I am." And with that he quieted and taught and solemnized the whole city. Now, in that again Socrates was God's dispensational apostle and preacher to the Greek people. For he was teaching them that there is, to begin with, no difference, that our hearts by nature are all equally evil, but that, as the Stoics taught, though all vice is equally in us all, it is not equally extant in us all. As also that he who knows his own heart will measure his own worth by his own heart and not by the valuation of the street and the market place. As also that the noblest and best men in all lands, and in all dispensations, are those who know themselves, and who out of that knowledge keep themselves under, and wait on God, till they attain in His good time to both a blameless heart, a blameless conscience, and a forever blameless life.

Yet another use of this solemn subject is for the comfort of the true people of God. It is to let them see that they are not alone, and that no strange thing is befalling them, in all they are passing through. For myself, when I hear Paul saying this that is in the text, and Luther, and Rutherford, and Bunyan, and Andrewes, and Edwards, and Brodie, it is with me as it was with John Bunyan's pilgrim in the valley of the shadow of death. "About the midst of the valley I perceived the mouth of hell to be, and it stood hard by the wayside, and ever and anon the flame and smoke, with sparks and noises, would come out in such abundance that Christian said, What shall I do? One thing I would not that you let slip. Just when he was come over against the mouth of the burning pit, one of the wicked ones got behind him, and stepped up softly to him, and whisperingly suggested many grievous blasphemies to him, which he verily thought had proceeded from his own mind. This put Christian more to it than anything he had met with before, yet could he have helped it, he would not have done it; but he had not the discretion either to stop his ears, or to know from whence these blasphemies came." And here comes our point: "When Christian had traveled in this disconsolate condition some considerable time, he thought he heard the voice of a man, as going before him, saying, Though I walk through the valley of the shadow of death, I will fear no evil, for thou art with me. Then was Christian glad, and that for these reasons: First, because he gathered from them that some who feared God were in the valley as well as himself. Secondly, for that he perceived God was with them, though in that dark and dismal state; and why not, thought he, with me? though by reason of the impediment that attends this place, I cannot perceive it. Thirdly, for that he hoped to have company by and by. So he went on, and called to him that was before; but he knew not what to answer, for that he also thought himself to be alone. And by and by the day broke. Then said Christian, He hath turned the shadow of death into the morning."

Paul as an Evangelical Mystic

THE TWO WORDS, "mystical" and "mysterious," mean very much the same thing. Not only so, but at bottom "mystical" and "mysterious" are very much the very same words. Like two sister stems, these two expressions spring up out of one and the same seminal root. Now, as to mysticism there are more kinds of mysticism than one in the world. There is speculative mysticism, and there is theosophical mysticism, and there is devotional mysticism, and so on. But to us there is only one real mysticism. And that is the evangelical mysticism of the Apostle Paul. And that mysticism is just the profound mysteriousness of the spiritual life, as that life was first created by the Holy Ghost in Jesus Christ, and forever will be possessed by Jesus Christ as His own original life, and then as forever it will be conveyed from Him down to all His mystical members.

Now, to begin with, Christ Himself is the great mystery of godliness. Almighty God never designed nor decreed nor executed anything in eternity or in time to compare, for one moment, to mysteriousness with Christ. All the mysteries of creation—and creation is as full as it can hold of all kinds of mysteries—and all the mysteries of grace—and grace is full of its own proper mysteries also—all are plain and easy to be understood, compared to the all-surpassing mystery of Christ. Ever since Christ was set forth among men all the best intellects in the world have been working on the mystery of Christ. And though they have found out enough of that mystery for their own salvation, yet they all agree in telling us that there are heights and depths of mystery in Christ past all finding out. Christ, then, that so mysterious Person who fills the Gospels and Epistles with His wonderful words and works, what think ye of Him? Paul tells us in every epistle of his what he thinks of Christ, and it is this deep, spiritual, experimental, and only soul-saving knowledge that Paul has of Christ—it is this that justifies us in calling him the first and the best of all mystics, the evangelical and true mystic, the only mystic, indeed, worthy for one moment to bear that deep and noble name.

When you take to reading the best books you will be sure to come continually on such strange descriptions and expressions as these: Christ mystical, Christ our mystical Head, Christ our mystical Root, the mystical Union of Christ with all true believers, the mystical identity of Christ with all true believers, and such like strange expressions. But already all these deep doctrines and strange expressions of evangelical mysticism are to be found in the deep places of Paul; and, in his measure, in the deep places of John also; and that because those two apostles, first of all spiritually-minded men, discovered all these mysterious and mystical matters in their Master. Ere ever we are aware, we ourselves are mystics as soon as we begin to read in John about the Living Bread and the True Vine, and in Paul about the Head of the Church and His indwelling in us. But Paul, after his great manner, goes on to show us that Christ is not the only mystical Head that this so mystically constituted world of ours has seen. First and last, as that great evangelical and speculative mystic has had it revealed to him, there have been two mystical Heads set over the human race. Our first mystical Head was Adam, and our second mystical Head is Christ. Speaking mystically, says the most mystical of the Puritans, there are only two men who stand before God, the first and the second Adam, and these two public Men have all us private men hanging at their great girdles. But all the time, above Adam, and before Adam, and only waiting till Adam had shipwrecked his headship and all who were in it with him, stood the second Adam ready to restore that which He had not taken away. And Paul so sets all that forth in doctrine, and in doxology, and in gospel invitation and assurance, that the Church of Christ in her gratitude to Paul has given him this great name of her first and most evangelical mystic. "And hath put all things under his feet," proclaims the great mystic, "and gave him to be the head over all things to the church, which is his body." And again, "him which is the head, even Christ, in whom the whole body maketh increase unto the edifying of itself in love." And again, "and he is the head of the body, for it pleased the Father that in him should all fulness dwell."

But while Paul has many magnificent things to teach us about the mystical Headship of Christ over His Church, at the same time it is the mystical union of Christ with each individual believer, and each individual believer's mystical union with Christ—it is this that completes and crowns Paul's evangelical doctrine and kindles his most rapturous adoration. And all that is so because all Paul's preaching is so profoundly experimental. Paul has come through all that he preaches. Goodwin, that so mystical and so evangelical Puritan, says that all the "apostolical and primitive language was at once mystical and experimental." But there is a more primitive and more experimental and a more mystical language than even the apostolic. "I am the bread of life: he that cometh to me shall never hunger; and he that believeth in me shall never thirst. This is the bread that cometh down from heaven, that a man may eat thereof and not die. Verily, verily, I say unto you, except ye eat the flesh of the Son of man and drink his blood, ye have no life in you." As also in our Lord's so mystical and so beautiful parable of the true vine and its true branches. And then in the next generation, Paul comes forward with his own so profound experience of all that, and with his own so first-hand witness to all that, in such sealing and crowning testimonies and attestations as these: "I live, yet not I, but Christ liveth in me: and the life I now live in the flesh, I live by the faith of the Son of God." And, again, "to me to live is Christ, and to die is gain," and so on in all his epistles. Paul has so eaten the flesh and has so drunk the blood of Christ, he has been of the Father so engrafted into Christ, that he is possessed by the risen Christ. The very identical life that is in Christ glorified is already in Paul, amid all his corruptions, temptations, and tribulations.

There are very different degrees of that life, to be sure, in Christ and in Paul; but it is the very same kind of life. There is not one kind of spiritual life in Christ and an altogether different kind of spiritual life in Paul. The same sap that is in the vine is in the branch. The same life that is in the head is in the member. But that is not all. Amazing as all that is, that is far from being all. The riches that are treasured up in Christ are absolutely unsearchable. For Paul is not content to say that he has in his own heart the identical and very same life that is in Christ's heart. Paul is bold enough to go on to say that he actually has Christ Himself dwelling in his very heart. You and I have in our hearts the very same life that was in Adam, with all its deadly infection and dreadful pollution; but, identified with Adam as we are, Adam does not really and actually dwell in our hearts. We still inherit the "fair patrimony" that he left us; but I, for one, both hope and believe that Adam has escaped that patrimony himself. At any rate, wherever Adam dwells, he does not dwell in our hearts. But the second Adam is so constituted for us, and we are so constituted for Him, that He, in the most real and actual manner, and without any figure of speech whatever, dwells in us. Indeed, with all reverence, and with all spiritual understanding, let it be said, Christ has no choice, He has nowhere else to dwell. If Christ is really to dwell, to be called dwelling, anywhere, it must be in Paul's heart, and in your heart, and in my heart. Christ is so mystical and mysterious, He is so unlike any one else in heaven or earth, He is such an unheard-of mystery, that He has *three* dwelling-places. To begin with, He is the Son of God, and as the Son of God He dwells in the Father, and the Father in Him. And then, ever since His Incarnation, He has been the Son of man also. And as the Son of man, and ever since His ascension and reception, He has dwelt in heaven as one of God's glorified saints, and at the head of them. But over and above being both Son of God and Son of man, from the mystical union of the Godhead and the manhood in His Divine Person He is the Christ also. And as He is the Christ, He dwells in His people, and can dwell nowhere, in heaven or in earth, but in His people. Christ mystical is made up, not of the Head only, but of the Head and the members taken together. And as apart from the Head the members have no life, so apart from His members nowhere has the Head to dwell. Nay, apart from His members, the Head has no real and proper existence. At any rate, as Paul insists, they are His fullness, and He is complete in and by them; just as they, again, are complete in and by Him. Paul, and you and I, hung, originally and in the beginning, at Adam's mystical girdle, and we all have had to take the consequences of that mystical suspension. But now we all have been loosed from Adam, and have been united close and inseparably to Christ. Before God, we all hang now at Christ's mystical girdle. Aye, far better, and far more blessed than even that, Christ now dwells under our girdle, and dwells, and can dwell, nowhere else. That is to say, in simple and plain language, He dwells in our hearts by faith and love on our part, and by mystical incorporation on His part. I am crucified with Christ, nevertheless I live, yet not I, but Christ liveth in me. And for this cause I bow my knees unto the Father of our Lord Jesus Christ, that Christ may dwell in your hearts by faith.

Now, as might be looked for, a thousand things, mystical and other, follow from all that, and will, to all eternity, follow from all that. But take one or two things that immediately and at once follow from all that, and so close this meditation. First, the mystical union between Christ and the soul is so mysterious that it is a great mystery even to those who are in it and share it. As Walter Marshall, one of the greatest doctors in this mystery, has it in his *Gospel Mystery*, "Yea, though it be revealed clearly in the Holy Scriptures, yet the natural man has not eyes to see it there. And if God expresses it never so plainly and properly, he will still think that God is speaking in riddles and parables. And I doubt not but it is still riddle, even to many truly godly men who have received a holy nature from God in this way. For the apostles themselves had the saving benefit of this mystery long before the Comforter had discovered it clearly to them. They walked in Christ as the way to the Father before they clearly knew Him to be the way. And the best of us know this mystery but in part and must wait for the perfect knowledge of it in another world." So mysterious is this mystery of godliness.

But how, asks some one honestly and anxiously—how shall I ever become such a miracle of Divine grace as to be actually, myself, a member of Christ's mystical body? Just begin at once to be one of His members, and the thing is done. Your hands do not hang idle and say, How shall we ever do any work? Your feet do not stand still and say, How shall we ever walk or run? Nor your eyes, nor your ears. They just begin to do, each, its proper work, and the moment they so begin, your head and your heart immediately send down their virtue into your hands and your feet. And so is it with the mystical Head and His mystical members. Just begin to be one of His members, and already you are one of them. Believe that you are one of them, and you shall be one of them. Just think about Christ. Just speak to Christ. Just lean on, and look to, Christ. Just go home tonight and do that deed of love, and truth, and humility, and brotherly kindness, and self-denial in His name, and already Christ is dwelling in you, and working in you as well as in Paul. Saul of Tarsus just said as he lay among his horse's feet, Lord, what wilt thou have me to do? And from that moment the thing was done.

Now, my brethren, if I have had any success tonight in setting forth Paul as an evangelical mystic, this also will follow as one of the many fruits of my argument. This fine word, "mystical," will henceforth be redeemed in all your minds from all that dreaminess, and cloudiness, and un-reality, and unpracticalness, with which it has hitherto been associated in your minds. "Vigor and efficacy" may not have been associated in many minds with the great mystical saints, and yet that is the very language that is used con-cerning them by no less an authority than Dr. Johnson. But just look at two or three of the greatest evangelical and saintly mystics for yourselves, and see if the great critic and lexicographer is not literally correct. Where are there vigor and efficacy in all the world like the vigor and efficacy of the Apostle Paul? Where is there less dreaminess or less cloudiness than in Paul? What a leader of men he was! What a founder and ruler of churches! What a man of busi-ness he was, and just that because of his mystical oneness with Christ! What an incomparably laborious, efficient, and fruitful life Paul lived! What a mystical conversation with heaven he kept up, combined with what stupendous serv-ices on earth! Take Luther also. There is not a more evan-gelically mystical book in all New Testament literature than Luther's *Galatians*. And yet, or I should rather say, and therefore, what truly Pauline vigor and efficacy in everything! And take Teresa and her mystical deacon always at her side, John of the Cross. I would need to be a genius at coining right words before I could describe aright to you that amazing woman's statesmanship and emperor-ship in life and in character. Founding schools, selecting sites, negotiating finances, superintending architects and builders and gardeners; always in the oratory, always on horseback. A mother in Israel. A queen among the most queenly women in all the world. And, unjust as Dr. Duncan is to William Law our greatest English mystic, Duncan is compelled to allow about Law that "he spoke upon the practical as with the sound of a trumpet. In practical appeals Law is a very Luther. Luther and Law were Boanerges." And, as Dr. Somerville, from whose fine book on Paul I have borrowed the title of this lecture, says, "The intensity that characterized the religious life and experience of the late General Gordon was all due to his evangelical mysticism. All associated in his case also with extraordinary efficiency in the practical affairs of life and in the management of men."

But why argue out such remote and historical instances when we have it all within ourselves? Let any man among ourselves carry Christ about in his own heart, let any man abide in Christ as the branch abides in the vine, let any man cleave as close to Christ as a member of our body cleaves close to its head, let any man say unceasingly every day, and in every cross and temptation of every day, "I am crucified with Christ: nevertheless I live, yet not I, but Christ liveth in me," and you will be absolutely sure to find that man the most willing, the most active, the most practical, and the most efficient man in every kind of Christian work. In one word, the more evangelically mystical any man is, the more full of all vigor and efficacy will that man be sure to be.

James Fraser

THE RELIGIOUS LITERATURE of Scotland is remarkably rich in books of religious autobiography. Telling us each one his own spiritual story we have James Melville, and Robert Blair, and John Livingstone, and Alexander Brodie, and James Fraser, and Thomas Halyburton, and Thomas Boston, and Hugh Miller, and John Duncan, and William Taylor, and Andrew Bonar. And there are not a few fragments of the same kind quite worthy to stand beside those full and finished works, such as the autobiographical remains of the Lady Coltness, the Lady Anne Elcho, and Marion Veitch. Every one of those famous autobiographies has its own individuality, idiosyncrasy, and physiognomy; and each one of them makes its own special contribution to the noblest catalogue of the books of our native land. I know something of all those great books; but there is none of them that draws me and holds me and keeps possession of me like the *Memoirs of Sir James Fraser of Brea, Written by Himself*. Dr. Jowett, writing to Lady Airlie, said that he had just finished Boswell for the fiftieth time, and Mr. Spurgeon was wont to say that he had read Bunyan a hundred times. I shall not attempt to count up the times I have read James Fraser of Brea, but if I did I feel sure that I would run both Jowett and Spurgeon hard.

Dr. Aird of Creich has collected the chief facts of Fraser's life into a short biographical sketch which will be found prefixed to the Inverness edition of Fraser's autobiography. And Dr. Elder Cumming of Glasgow has an admirable appreciation of Fraser in his *Holy Men of God*. The following are the main outlines of Fraser's much-tried life. He was born at Brea, his father's estate in Ross-shire, on the 29th of July, 1639. His father died while his son James was still a child, and some of his greatest troubles in life came to him out of his ownership of that estate. Although he began to study for the legal profession, young Fraser eventually gave himself up to the study of divinity, to which he brought a mind of the first intellectual order. From his earliest days the Laird of Brea identified himself with the outed evangelical ministers of the north, and all along he was a most pronounced Presbyterian and Covenanter, and both by his tongue and by his pen fought unflinchingly for the freedom of his Church and his country. Both in the Bass and in Blackness and in Newgate he suffered the most unjust imprisonment, and the wickedest and the most malicious illusage. After the Revolution we find Fraser settled as parish minister of Culross, where he closed his troubled career about the year 1698. Dr. Aird adds this note to his short sketch of Fraser's life: "He was assisted at a communion at Culross, very shortly before his death, by the celebrated Boston of Ettrick, then a young man."

But with all that it is in his *Memoirs of Himself* that James Fraser of Brea will live, and he will live in that remarkable book as long as a scholarly religion, and an evangelical religion, and a spiritual religion, and a profoundly experimental religion lives in his native land. In saying that I do not forget the warning that Dr. Elder Cumming gives me to the effect that Fraser's will be a Scottish reputation only, and even that will be limited to readers of a special cast of religious experience and spiritual sympathy. At the same time, Dr. Elder Cumming adds that Fraser's autobiography is a book that for depth and for grip has a few, if any, equals among the foremost books of its kind in the whole world.

Now, you will naturally ask me at this point just what

it is that gives James Fraser such a high rank as a spiritual writer, and just what it is that so signalizes his *Memoirs of Himself*. Well, in his own characteristic words, his *Memoirs* is "the book of the intricacies of his own heart and life," and that on their purely spiritual side. Now, Fraser's mind was by nature of the most intricate kind, that is to say, his mind was naturally of the most acute and subtle and penetrating and searching-out kind. Had he gone into law, as at one time he intended to do, he would infallibly have taken rank as one of the acutest of our Scottish lawyers. And with his immense industry he would to a certainty have left writings behind him that would have been of classical authority in that great profession. But to the lasting enrichment of his own soul, and to the lasting enrichment of all his kindred-minded readers' souls, Fraser was led of God into divinity, and into divinity of the deepest, acutest, most evangelical, and most experimental kind. "I chose divinity," says Butler, "it being of all studies the most suitable to a reasonable nature."

Unhappily for us, many of Fraser's private journals, family papers, and estate documents are hopelessly lost. But if ever they are recovered I feel sure it will be found that he had made out more than once a most exact map and inventory of his inherited estate with his own exact and intricate hands. I can see the delineaments and the depictments of the whole estate of Brea as they were laid down by the honestest, and the exactest, and the intricatest of pens. I can see its hills and its glens, its farms and its crofts, its streams and its lochs, its cattle and its games and its fish, all laid down with a mathematical exactness and a geometrical completeness as if he were preparing his estate for the Inverness or Edinburgh market, and as if he were determined to do so with the most absolute justice to both the seller and the buyer. Now, whether those maps and plans and accompanying documents are ever recovered or no, most happily we have some still more important documents preserved to us from Fraser's faithful and careful hands. I refer to the delineations he made of the inward estate of his own soul, a delineation and an inventory that has been preserved to us to this day, I will say, under the special and adorable providence of Fraser's God and our God. And it is an analysis and a delineation and a depictment of such a kind that I know nothing to approach it in any language that I read. And I thank God every day that so intricate and so spiritual a book is not in Hebrew or Greek or Latin, but is in my own Scottish tongue wherein I was born. Fraser describes his spiritual autobiography as "The Book of the Intricacies of his own Heart and Life." And so it is. It is a book of such intricacy and sinuosity and complication and reticulation and involution that in all my experience of such books it stands simply unparalleled and unapproached. No labyrinth ever constructed by the brain of man comes near the heart of Brea. Not even that wonder of the world the labyrinth of Egypt, with its three thousand secret chambers. Not even the Cretan labyrinth of Daedalus, with its bloodthirsty monster at its center, and with only a thin linen thread to lead you out through its endless tortuosities to the open air. All that is but a faint and feeble description of the always spiritually intricate book that Fraser of Brea has bequeathed to his fellow countrymen and his fellow churchmen. To as many of them, that is, as have an intricate life of their own, and a labyrinthine heart of their own. And among the thousands of his Christian fellow countrymen in our day there must surely be some men still left with something of the intellectual strength, and the spiritual inwardness, and the experimental concentration, and the holy fear and the close walk with God, of the Laird of Brea. Some men who will feel that they are not such absolute monsters among men, and so much alone in Scotland, as they always thought they were till they were told about James Fraser, the Laird of Brea. Well may Dr. Elder Cumming say that Brea's is a book to be read by all men with wonder and with awe; and, I will add, to be read by some men with an ever-increasing thankfulness and an ever-increasing hopefulness. Yes, well might his old publisher in first venturing Brea's autobiography out on the market go on to say: "There is perhaps no other Performance giving a more distinct Account of a supernatural Work of Grace. And it is thought not to be unseasonable at this juncture for reviving Piety and the Exercise of Grace, and convicting those who make a jest of these serious Matters."

Now, in summing up all I have already said about Fraser and his autobiography, I will say a single word here about the immense importance of intellect in our evangelical preachers and experimental writers. And instead of any weak words of my own on that matter, take these so fresh and so pointed words of Santa Teresa: "I always had a great respect and affection for intellectual and learned men," she says. "It is my experience that all who intend to be true Christians will do well to treat with men of mind when they are being deeply exercised about their souls. The more intellect and the more learning our preachers and pastors have, the better. The devil is exceedingly afraid of learning, especially when it is accompanied with great humility and great virtue. Let no one be taken into this religious house of ours unless she is a woman of a sound understanding. For if she is without mind, she will neither know herself nor will she understand her best teachers. And ignorance and self-conceit is a disease that is simply incurable. And, besides, it usually carries great malice and great malignity along with it. Commend me to people with good heads. From all silly devotees may God deliver me!" Had Santa Teresa lived in Scotland in the seventeenth century she would to a certainty have taken a house at Culross in order to sit under Fraser's ministry. Nay, she would to a certainty have taken service as a scullery maid on the Bass Rock just to be under the same roof with a man of such learning and such intellect in his religion, and a man, at the same time, of such a broken heart in his daily devotions.

And, then, one of the best of intellects of that intellectual day is here to be seen employed, exclusively and unceasingly, on what its owner conceived to be the best, the noblest, and the most commanding of all occupations—the salvation of his own soul, and in and after that the same salvation of other men's souls. Let a man constantly examine himself on that supreme matter, says the Apostle. Well, James Fraser has only one fault in that respect: he takes the Apostle much too seriously and much too literally, for he is always and in everything examining himself. Whether Paul would have praised Fraser or blamed him for that incessant introspection of his, you have your opinion, and I have mine. Watch and pray, says our Lord also. Well, did any of the twelve do that like the Laird of Brea? No, I am quite sure that none of them did—not, at any rate, to begin with. "My people do not consider," complained the God of covenanted Israel. Now, our complaint here again with Fraser is this, that he considered too much, and that he would do nothing else all his days but consider inwardly and then act outwardly. Fraser believed with all his deep mind and with all his renewed heart that there was but one thing absolutely and supremely necessary as between him and his God, and he wrote his book and lived his life accordingly. In season and out of season, Fraser of Brea pursued that one thing with an intricacy, and with a tenacity, and with a perspicuity unparalleled in all my reading or hearing of such men and such matters.

And then I have this also for my defense and apology in taking up such an out-of-date man—Fraser of Brea is one of ourselves. He is one of our own covenanted household of faith. He is one of our own cloud of witnesses. "People are variously constituted," says Dr. Newman in an exquisite essay. "What I delight to trace and to study," he says, "is the interior life of God's great saints. And when a great saint himself speaks to me about himself, that is what I like best, and that is what is done by those early luminaries of the Christian Church, Athanasius, and Hilary, and Ambrose, and Theodoret. This is why I exult in the folios of the Fathers. I am not obliged to read the whole of them. I read what I can, and am content." And if I may be bold enough to borrow that from Newman, I shall be loyal enough to apply that to myself and to say that that is the very same reason why I so exult in Bunyan, and in Baxter, and in Goodwin, and in Brea, and in Halyburton, and in Boston, and in Chalmers—a body of men who, as Coleridge has it, are, for the matter in hand, worth a whole brigade of the Fathers. At the same time, I do not forget that people are very variously constituted. What influences one does not in the same way influence another. Nor am I obliged to read the whole of our evangelical and experimental and Puritan Fathers. I read what I can, and am content; or, rather, I for one exult —and then, as a wise old writer has it, "the judicious are fond of originals." And then, as to the reward that we may confidently look for from our study of Fraser's autobiography. In his dedication to Thomas Ross of Tain, our author says: "I have in nothing been more refreshed, quickened, and edified than by hearing and reading of the experiences of others of God's people, and in nothing more comforted and sanctified than by a serious recalling to mind of the Lord's intricate dealings with myself." And far on in the body of the book he returns to that subject, and says: "The calling to mind and seriously meditating on the Lord's secret dealings with myself as to soul and body; my recalling of His manifold and intimate mercies to me has done me very much good; has cleared my case; has confirmed my soul concerning God's love to me, and of my interest in Him;

and has made me love Him more and more. O what good hath the writing of this book of my *Memoirs* done me! What wells of water have mine eyes been opened to see that before were hid from me! Scarce anything hath done me more good than the writing of this book!" And I will say that scarce anything hath done the writer of this Appreciation more good than the reading of such chapters in this book as these: I, IV, VI, XIII, XVI, XVIII, XX, XXIV, and three times as many and all as good, till this line about a great man in a very different dispensation comes to my mind, "Probed many hearts, beginning with his own."

Thomas Shepard

JONATHAN EDWARDS, "one of the greatest of the sons of men," has given us his Appreciation of Thomas Shepard in a most eloquent and impressive way. I know no such complete and conclusive appreciation in all literature as when Jonathan Edwards on every page underbuilds and establishes and illustrates his spiritual masterpiece, the *Religious Affections,* with constant reference to the *Ten Virgins,* the *Sound Convert* and the *Spiritual Experiences,* with no less than innumerable quotations from those so experimental Puritan books. I know no instance of the *laudatur a laudato* principle at all to compare with that of Thomas Shepard and Jonathan Edwards. Now, though I cannot speak with an atom of authority of Edwards, at the same time I am not on that account wholly shut out from making my own humble acknowledgment of what I also owe to this great Pilgrim Father. I am not debarred from laying my own loyal tribute at the feet of the man on whose head Jonathan Edwards has set such a crown.

Thomas Shepard has been one of my favorite authors ever since the year 1861, when my honored friend, Dr. Williamson of Huntly, wrote my name on his own copy of the *Parable of the Ten Virgins.* I think I must have read Shepard quite as often as Spurgeon had read Bunyan, quite as often at any rate as Jowett had read Boswell. And I am still reading Shepard as if I had never read him before. As a proof of that take this little confidence of mine. The week before one of my holidays I had read Professor Churton Collins' delightful paper on *The Tempest* that had appeared some time previously in the *Contemporary Review*. And so impressed was I with the learned professor's paper that I took to the country with me Dr. Furness's variorum and monumental edition of that exquisite work, promising myself a great revel over the great text and over the extraordinary rich mass of explanatory and illustrative notes. But—would you believe it?—with such a temptation lying on my table all the time I never once opened the seductive volume. For, as God would have it, as John Bunyan was wont to say, I had taken Thomas Shepard also with me, and I read the *Ten Virgins,* and the *Sincere Believer,* and the *Sound Convert,* and the *Saint's Jewel,* and the *Select Cases,* and the *Spiritual Experiences* over and over again—execrable English and all. And instead of repenting myself for my neglect of Shakespeare and his monumental editor, I came home thanking God again for His so notable and so exceptional servant Shepard. And, more than that, I came home more settled and resolved than ever to do all I can to make you know something of Shepard's matchlessly pungent lessons in spiritual and experimental religion. And to reassure me I took out of my desk and read again a postcard bearing the Aberdeen post mark, which I received some years ago and which runs thus: "A thousand thanks for pressing Thomas Shepard on our attention. After long looking for it, I have at last got a copy of the *Parable,* and I can scarcely lay it down. It is proving itself a very book of life to me. This is the preaching that our day needs.—A Free Church Minister."

I dare say you will remember that I was always besieging you to buy and to read all your days, as also to distribute, the *Pilgrim's Progress* and the *Grace Abounding*. But you will have perfect peace of mind concerning Thomas Shepard and his works. For I shall never ask any of you to spend one penny on Shepard, such is his atrocious English. Bunyan and Shepard are at one in the deepest things, but they stand at opposite poles in the matter of their English style. Shepard at his very best wrote an all but unrecognizable English. But after the New England printers and then the Aberdeen printers had put Shepard's best book through their hands, if hands they could be called, Shepard came forth absolutely unreadable, unless to a few resolved and relentless and irresistible readers, such as Mrs. Black of Dunnikier Manse, and R. Foote of Brechin, and Dr. Williamson, and myself. Much as I respect William Greenhill's judgment, I cannot follow him when he says of Shepard that "here is a cornfield without cockle or thorns or thistles." I know quite well what Greenhill means when he says all that, and I wholly subscribe to his deep meaning. But if I were to repeat his words without some warning, you might be led into advertising for the old book, which you would no sooner open than you would throw it down in disgust and in indignation both at Shepard and at Greenhill and at me. "Polybius," says Dr. Butcher, "pays the penalty attaching to neglect of form; he is read by few." At the same time I will say this: As we find Principal Rendall quite frankly acknowledging the heavy cramped vocabulary, and the deadness of expression, and the formless monotony of clause that all combine to weigh down the *First Book* of Marcus Aurelius, while at the same time he stands up against Matthew Arnold when that critic says that the Emperor's style lacks distinction and physiognomy, so will I stand up for Shepard's distinction and for his physiognomy. The truth is, while repeating and exaggerating all the stoic Emperor's faults of style, Shepard's mental countenance is even more unmistakable to me than is that of the royal author of the immortal *Thoughts*. There is no possibility of our ever mistaking a page or a paragraph or even a sentence of Thomas Shepard's. Not only because of its Paul-like hands and feet. For Shepard, once he has got on your track, will follow hard after you all your days. And once he gets a real hold of you, as Luther said of Paul, you will never be able to shake him off again. But when all is said that can be said about Shepard's sluggard's-garden of a style, if you will go with me into the resolved study of this great Puritan I will promise you many a sweet and fragrant flower out of his crannied and crumbling walls, and many a medicinal herb out of his stoniest places, and many a cup of wine well refined out of his most gnarled or crabbed vine-stocks. Just gird up your loins and come with me and see if it will not be so. And as the saintly David Brainerd says, "We shall see what passed for soul-saving religion with that so excellent and so venerable Pilgrim Father Thomas Shepard, the author of the *Sound Convert,* the *Spiritual Experiences,* and the *Parable Unfolded."*

Take these, then, as some specimen and characteristic headings, sometimes of short entries, and sometimes of whole chapters, in Shepard's *Spiritual Experiences*: "No one who ever came under my shadow prospered." "The more I do, the worse I am." "My idle words in my preaching, in my praise, and in my prayer." "The sins of one day I forget the next day." "I come to see that God is having His whole Name in Exodus 34 fulfilled and adorned in me." "For His sake I am killed all the day long." "I keep a private fast for the conquest of my pride." "My sins are sometimes crucified, but they are never mortified." "I am salted with suffering." *"Fiat experimentum in corpore vili"* ("I abhor myself"). "You ask me what cured me of being an infidel." "Some remorses of an old ministry." "Surely I have always laid my pipe far short of the Fountain," and so on, through the whole unique book. Now, I will appeal to all readers of the best literature to say if they ever came on more penetrating and more pungent titles and topics than these. At any rate, the immortal author of the *Freedom of the Will,* and the *True Virtue,* and the *Religious Affections* never did; and his splendid appreciation of Thomas Shepard runs accordingly.

When matters were not going well with Shepard himself

in his family life, in his pain and remorse he would sometimes say that he thought the Pope had the right way of it
with his preachers and pastors. At any rate, he would sometimes say, I wish I had remained a celibate along with my
own soul all my days. Other men, he was wont to say, might
not always manage their family life with the most perfect
success, but a minister's breakdown at home was to Shepard
the greatest of all domestic tragedies. He had known many
ministers, in both Old England and New England, whose
family life was a great success in every way. But not his
own. As for himself, neither wife, nor child, nor servant,
nor visitor prospered spiritually under his baleful shadow.
So he enters it, again and again, on occasions, in his secret
journal which he kept alone with God. Nobody but himself thought such things about Thomas Shepard. All the
same, never was there more sincerity or more poignancy in
any private journal than there was in his. Thales was so
fond of children that nothing would persuade him to become a father. And though Thomas Shepard became the
father of more children than one, he both loved and pitied
his children so much that he would sometimes wish they
had never been born, at any rate to him.

Altogether, substitute Thomas Shepard, the new England
Puritan, for Santa Teresa, the Spanish Superior, and you
will have his exact case in his home life, as he so often saw
and felt it to be. Thomas Shepard could not express himself
nearly so well as Santa Teresa could; but in substance and
in essence they both said exactly the same thing. "My children," said the saint on her deathbed, "you must pardon me
much. You must pardon me most of all the bad example I
have given you. Do not imitate me. Do not live as I have
lived. I have been the greatest sinner in all Spain. I have
not kept the laws that I laid down for other people. But,
then, is not this written in David expressly for me, The sacrifices of God are a broken spirit; a broken and contrite

heart God will not despise"? Thomas Shepard and Teresa of Jesus would not have spoken to one another on earth. But they are now praising God together in glory; and for their family shame they are now having the double as they sing together before the throne, and say: "By Thy great grace to us, O God, here are we ourselves, and all the children that Thou didst give us."

When Dr. Chalmers was out at Stirling on one occasion he went to the village school and gave the children an elementary lesson in optical science. Taking the blackboard and a piece of chalk, he drew a long diameter on the board, and then he ran a large circumference around the diameter. And then turning to the wondering children he said to them in his own imaginative and eloquent way, "You must all see that the longer the diameter of light the larger is the surrounding circumference of darkness." Now, all we have to do in order to explain and illustrate one of Thomas Shepard's most startling self-accusations is to carry over Dr. Chalmers' mathematical and optical blackboard into the region of moral and spiritual things. "The more I do," says Shepard oftener than once, "the worse I am." That is to say, the longer the diameter of Shepard's duty done, the larger is the circumference of duty he still has to do. And the holier and holier his heart and life become, the more sinful the remaining corruption of his heart and life becomes to him, till he is constrained to cry out with the holiest of men, "O wretched man that I am!"

And then, carrying up all his own experience of the spiritual life therewith to deepen and strengthen and enrich his pulpit work, the great preacher would say: "There is no difference. I am as you are, and you are as I am. Just try the thing yourselves. Just begin to love God with all your heart, and you will soon see that the more you try to do that, the less will you feel satisfied that you succeed. And, in like manner, when you begin to love your neighbor as yourself you will begin to get a lesson with a vengeance in the spiritual life. Just try to rejoice in all your neighbor's well-being as much as you rejoice in your own. Just try to relish and enjoy all other men's praises of your neighbor as you relish and enjoy all other men's praises of yourself. Just try to take delight in all your neighbor's rewards, promotions, prosperities as you take delight in your own. And go on trying to do that toward all men around you, friend and foe, and you will get a lesson in the infinite and exquisite holiness and spirituality of God's law of love, and at the same time a lesson in the abominable and unspeakable corruptions of your own heart that will make you wiser in all these matters than all your teachers." In such home-coming homiletic as that Shepard made pulpit and pastoral application of his own experiences in the spiritual life, till he became a foremost master in all these holy matters, and till men like Edwards and Brainerd sat as his scholars at his feet in New England, and till his name became a tower of truth and power in the Old England from which he had been exiled.

Walter Marshall and His Book, *The Gospel—Mystery of Sanctification*

WILLIAM COWPER writes thus in one of his classical letters: "The book you mention lies now on my table. Marshall is an old acquaintance of mine. I think Marshall one of the best writers, and one of the most spiritual expositors of Scripture I ever read. I never met a man who understood the plan of salvation better, or who was more happy in explaining it to others." And James Hervey, the well-known author of *Theron and Aspasio,* says of Marshall's book: "It has been one of the most useful books to my own soul. I scarce ever fail to receive spiritual consolation and strength from the perusal of it. And was I to be banished into some desolate island, possessed of only two books besides my Bible, this should be one of the two, perhaps the very first I would choose." The saintly Robert Trail also says: "Mr. Marshall was a holy and retired man, known only to the world by this one book, which is deep, practical, well-connected, and requiring a more than ordinary attention to read it with profit. Its great excellence is that it leads the serious reader directly and immediately to Jesus Christ." And Adam Gib of Edinburgh used to say of Marshall: "I have scarcely ever been acquainted with any practical treatise of human product so evangelical, in a thread more correct and a method more exact than this." "Did I ever speak to you about Marshall on sanctification?" asks Dr. Chalmers. "He is at present my daily companion." And Dr. Andrew Murray of South Africa says in his introduction to a most excellent abridgment of Marshall: "There is but one book in the English language admitted by all to be the standard book on sanctification. It is the work of the Rev. Walter Marshall, published in 1692. It has at all times received the highest praise from men of eminence, both as theologians and saints." And Dr. Elder Cumming once said to the present writer: "Ah! Walter Marshall is just Keswick for theologians and men of mind." And Dr. Laidlaw, in a like conversation: "Marshall is simply the last word on the subject."

Walter Marshall's one book is but a small book in bulk, and his life his book. He was born in 1638. He was educated at Oxford. He was settled in Hursley. He declared for Presbytery. He was cast out of his parish. He profited greatly himself by his preaching; from its efficacy on his own heart he attained to very uncommon degrees of faith and holiness and comfort. He had been for long in great darkness as to the way of attaining to true holiness and true peace. He consulted Richard Baxter and Thomas Goodwin, among others. After he had confessed to Goodwin many sins in his heart and in his life, Goodwin replied, "You have forgotten to mention the greatest sin of all. The great sin of not believing on the Lord Jesus Christ both for the remission of sins and for holiness of heart."

In reading such authors as Hooker, and Leighton, and Owen, and Goodwin, and Rutherford, and Edwards, we continually come on this expression, the mystical union. Now, that is a theological and an experimental expression. The thing is in the Scriptures, though not the exact words. The Scriptures, indeed, are full of the thing. And that so expressive phrase has been coined by our great evangelical theologians in order to convey to the mind a certain picture of that glorious relationship which is constituted between Christ and the soul, when the soul is once truly united to Christ, and is, as it were, incorporated into Christ. Now, Paul is the great apostle of the mystical union. The mystical union is in every epistle of his. It might almost be said that the mystical union is in every chapter of his. For Christ and the believer in Christ is Paul's constant theme. We are chosen in Christ before the foundation of the world. We are accepted in the Beloved. It hath pleased the Father that in Him should all fullness dwell. And ye are complete in Him, for in Him dwelleth all the fullness of the Godhead bodily. Rooted and built up in Him, we are to grow up into Him in all things, which is the Head, even Christ. Compared with Christ and the mystical union of believers with Christ, Paul as good as knows nothing, either in his preaching or in his epistles. And in this Marshall is a "right Pauline divine," as Luther says. This is what Dr. Murray says on this subject: "In chapter three Marshall teaches us how in Jesus Christ a new nature was prepared for the believer, how the needed endowments for living holily are provided for in that new nature, and how this is communicated to us through our living union with Christ. The beauty of Marshall's book is that he makes the Mystical Union the starting point in the Christian course. He points out how by faith the sinner receives Christ and His salvation, how justification and sanctification are both given in Christ and received only through the faith that unites to Him. In our union to Christ, realized by faith from day to day, and in each duty we perform, is the only, but the sufficient, strength for a holy life." And Dr. Murray adds, "Let me in conclusion urge every believer who longs to understand better the secret of a holy life to take time for the study of this little book. He need be afraid of no new doctrine, though the distinctness and the point may make it appear new. But let no one imagine that a hasty reading of this book will do him any good. Let him return and read more than once or twice, till mind and heart become familiarized with the blessed truth of a sinner on earth living and speaking and acting daily and hourly as a saint, and that in the power of a holiness dwelling in heaven, because the life of Jesus is his life. And I cannot but think that such a reader will find our writer to be indeed God's messenger to guide him into God's highway of holiness, and into a life of peace and power before unknown." Walter Marshall has found an editor worthy of himself in Andrew Murray.

And now, to close with, take one or two of Marshall's many striking sentences that arrest us in the course of our reading of *The Gospel—Mystery of Sanctification.*

On the law of love he says incidentally, "Take notice, that the law which is your mark, is exceeding broad, and yet not the more easy to be hit, because you must aim to hit it in every duty of it, with a performance of equal breadth, or else you do not hit it at all." And his whole argument revolves round such a passage as this: "Many men who are seriously devout take a great deal of pains to mortify their corrupted nature by pressing vehemently on their hearts many motives to holiness; laboring importunately to squeeze good affections out of their hearts, as oil out of a flint. On this account they think the entrance into holy life to be harsh and unpleasing, because it costs so much struggling with their evil hearts to new-frame them. If only they knew that this way of entrance into a holy life is not only harsh and unpleasant, but altogether impossible, and that the true way to mortify sin and quicken their hearts to holiness is by receiving a new nature out of the fullness of Christ, and that we do no more to the production of a new nature than to the production of original sin, though we do more to the reception of it—if only they knew this, they might save themselves many a bitter agony, and employ their endeavors to enter in at the strait gate in such a way as would be far more pleasant and successful." And again, "The old man, the body of sin, is destroyed in us, not by any wounds that we ourselves can give to it, but by our partaking of that freedom from it, that death unto it, that is already wrought out for us by the death of Christ. Therefore we must be content to leave the natural man vile and wicked, as we found it, until it be utterly destroyed by death, though we must not allow its wickedness." And again, "Nature remains wicked, and only wicked, even after we have put on Christ." And again, "As our natural corruption was produced originally in the first Adam, and was propagated from him to us: so our new nature is produced first in Christ, and is derived from Him to us: or, as it were, propagated." And to wind up, "Christ would have us believe on Him that justifieth the ungodly, and therefore He doth not require us to be godly before we believe. He came as a physician to the sick, and He does not expect that they shall recover their health in the least degree before they come to Him. The vilest sinners are fitly prepared and qualified for this design, which is to show forth the exceeding riches of grace. For this end the law of Moses entered, that the offense might abound, so that, where sin abounded, grace might much more abound."

Our Lord and the Bible

*And there was delivered unto him the book of the
prophet Esaias.*

FAMILY BIBLES were as universal in Israel as ever they were
in Scotland. The time was when no new household was ever
set up in Scotland without a family Bible being found
among its marriage presents. And Joseph and Mary, you
may depend on it, did not start on their married life without having the Word of God laid out at the head of their
most highly prized marriage possessions. And even if a
complete and costly scribe-written Bible was not to be seen
in every young carpenter's house in Nazareth, Mary would
be of the mind of her first-born Son who said long afterwards to His disciples, "But now he that hath a purse, let
him take it, and likewise his scrip; and he that hath no
sword, let him sell his garment, and buy one." It was of
their family Bible that the God of Israel spoke to His covenant people, and said, "And those words of mine shall be
in thine heart. And thou shalt talk of them when thou sit-
test in thine house, and when thou walkest by the way, and
when thou liest down, and when thou risest up. And thou
shalt bind them for a sign upon thine hand, and they shall
be as frontlets between thine eyes. And thou shalt write
them upon the posts of thy house, and on thy gates." And
was there a house in all Israel, from first to last, high or low,
rich or poor, learned or simple, where that commandment
concerning the family Bible, and concerning family wor-

ship, was so sure to be observed as just in that house into which God sent His Son Jesus Christ to be born and brought up? To this day, when Almighty God has any future servant of His to be born and brought up among ourselves, He selects, as a rule, a house where there is a sanctified Sabbath, and a family Bible, and family worship. "And thou shalt show thy son in that day, saying, This is done because of that which the Lord did unto me when I came forth out of Egypt, that the Lord's law may be in thy mouth." And in this way this Evangelist, who had perfect understanding of all things from the very first, might with perfect propriety and with entire safety have said to us that the Book of God, His Heavenly Father, was delivered to the Holy Child Jesus as soon as He was able to hold it in His hand.

And then, to borrow His own words, our Lord "searched the Scriptures" from the days of His earliest youth till He discovered that they testified of Himself. Coleridge was wont to say that the Scriptures so "found" him that he was compelled to confess their divinity. And Halyburton has a memorable confession in his *Memoirs* to the same effect. And may it not be said with the most perfect truth that our Lord both found Himself in the Holy Scriptures and that they found Him? For never before or since were the Scriptures searched as they were searched by Jesus, both child and man. And never did such discoveries reward any other searcher as His discoveries rewarded Him. For He discovered Himself in the Scriptures, and then He discovered Himself by means of them. Holy Scripture was the golden key by means of which Jesus of Nazareth entered into, and took possession of, that mystery of godliness which was Himself. He saw Himself as in a glass in every page of Holy Scripture. As He said Himself, Moses and all the prophets testified of Him, and He came to the full knowledge of Himself by hearkening to their testimony, by searching into their testimony, and by receiving their testimony. "I have no books," said a poor, but princely minded servant of His, "but I have myself." And Jesus of Nazareth had no books beyond His Bible and Himself, but He read in those two great books of God till they became one Book in His hand. David had searched the Scriptures in a wonderful way and to a wonderful enjoyment. But David's Son excelled David in all other Scripture searchers who had gone before Him. With far greater depth and strength and thankfulness than David ever attained to, David's son took David's words out of His father's mouth and made them all His own. "Thou, through thy commandments, hast made me wiser than mine enemies, for they are ever with me. I have more understanding than all my teachers; for thy testimonies are my meditation. I understand more than the ancients, because I keep thy precepts." For never did Moses, or David, or Isaiah, or any other psalmist or prophet in all the house of Israel, search into and meditate on Holy Scripture as did Jesus of Nazareth, and never were its precepts kept to such an illumination, to such a revelation, and to such a glorious reward. With what an unfathomable depth of awe and wonder did Jesus search into the Scriptures concerning Himself! And with what boundless adoration and praise did He more and more discover and find Himself in them! "O how I love thy law!" He exclaimed. "It is my meditation all the day. The statutes of the Lord are right, rejoicing the heart; the commandment of the Lord is pure, enlightening the eyes. More to be desired are they than gold, yea, than much gold; sweeter also than honey and the honeycomb."

Now, my brethren, that very same Book has been delivered to you and to me from our youth up. And along with it a fuller, a clearer and a much richer Book. The complete and finished Book of God, Old Testament and New, has been delivered to us to see what we will make of it. To see

how we will search it, and what we will find in it, and in
ourselves by means of it, and then all that will infallibly decide what we are and what we will make of ourselves, and
where we will find ourselves at last. All the other books in
this wide world taken together do not for one moment
concern us in comparison with this Book. For the whole
meaning and purpose and true end and design of our whole
existence, as of our Lord's existence; all our Maker's purpose
and intention in our creation, preservation, and redemption; our chief end on earth, and our endless enjoyment of
God in heaven—all that is here, and is nowhere else. "In Cicero, and Plato, and other such writers," says St. Augustine,
"I meet with many things acutely said, and things that
excite a certain warmth of emotion, but in none of them do
I find such words as these: 'Come unto me, all ye that labor,
and are heavy laden, and I will give you rest.'" When the
Book was delivered that day to our Lord He soon found the
place in the prophet Isaiah where it was written of Him.

Now, you have all had that same prophet delivered to you
all your days. Well, have you up to this day found any of
the places where Isaiah has written of you? For example,
have you found for yourself these two places about yourself?
First this: "The whole head is sick, and the whole heart
faint. From the sole of the foot even unto the head there is
no soundness in you, but wounds, and brusies, and putrify-
ing sores." And then this: "We are all as a unclean thing,
and all our righteousnesses are as filthy rags." Isaiah had
found all that in himself long before he wrote it down
about himself, and about Israel, and about us. If he had not
found all that, and all that every day in himself, he would
never have had the boldness to set it down first about Israel and then about us. And then it was his continual finding of all that in himself that led him on to find Christ crucified in Moses and in the prophets till he became wiser
than all his teachers in his famous fifty-third chapter. It

was because Isaiah was such a woeful man to himself that he became such an evangelical minister to us. Woe is me! for I am undone, he cried in the Temple. But that moment the live coal from off the altar touched his lips, till he was sent to preach Christ as Christ was never preached before or since, till Paul also found himself in the same Scripture, and cried out, O wretched man that I am! And exactly so was it with Thomas Halyburton, that spiritual genius, first of Ceres and then of St. Andrews: "All discoveries of guilt were conveyed by the Scriptures. God spake by the Scriptures in mine ear of sins which God alone could know; God who searches the heart. By the Scriptures the secrets of my heart were made manifest; and hereon I could not but fall down and own that God was in His word of a truth. And now I was ready to say, Come, and see a Book that has told me all that ever I did in my life; is not this the Book of God? And it was by the same Book that He let in upon my soul His whole will as to my salvation by Jesus Christ. Herein it was that He declared His name—the Lord God, merciful and gracious unto sinners in Christ."

"Beginning at Moses and all the prophets, He expounded unto them in all the Scriptures the things concerning himself," till their hearts burned within them. And that is the true way still. We preachers also will make men's hearts to burn within them when we expound to them the Scriptures concerning ourselves. Experience is the true exegete in Holy Scripture, said Luther. Weep yourself, said the old Roman instructor, and you will soon make me weep in sympathy with you. Yes, all you who are candidates to be expounders of the Scriptures, search the Scriptures till you find yourselves in them as nowhere else. You have doubts and difficulties about this and that in Holy Scripture. Or rather, less about things in the Scriptures than about things that lie outside of and round about the Scriptures. Doubts and difficulties about the paper the Scriptures are printed on, about the ink with which they are printed, about their binding, and about who bound them up in the way they are bound up. Read Halyburton, and then search the Scriptures as he searched them, and your salad doubts and difficulties will soon disappear.

"O fools," their Master said to those disciples of His who had failed to search the Scriptures for the things concerning their Master and themselves—"O fools, ought not Christ to have suffered these things, and to enter into his glory?" They had neglected that search, and thus it was that both His sufferings and theirs took them unawares and found them slow of heart to believe. Whereas He had searched the Scriptures from His manger to His cross, and from His cross to His throne, till He was able to meet all these things well prepared and waiting for them all. Let us be like Him. We have the same Scriptures, let us have the same mind. And if we search the Scriptures with His same mind we also shall find written there all our intervening sufferings and all our future glory, till we shall, like Him, be able now to rebuke and now to console those who weep over us, and those who charge God foolishly, and say to them that all this is but what we foresaw from the beginning, that the trial of our faith, being much more precious than of gold that perisheth, though it be tried with fire, may be bound unto praise, and honor, and glory at the appearing of Jesus Christ. Let us search the Scriptures, like our Lord, for all these things, and then enter into our promised rest.

O my brethren, since all these things are so, what a day that is for you and for him when you deliver to your son his first Bible! What a treasure house of unsearchable riches you that day put into his hand! What a lifelong search he has before him from that day! And a deeper and deeper search every day he lives, till that day when, like Thomas Boston's dying elder, he will lay his hand on his greatest earthly possession and say to it as he forever parts with it,

Farewell the Bible! And, then, the written word will immediately be exchanged by him for the Living and the Eternal Word. And till the earthly sanctuary, where you and he searched the Scriptures together with your minister will hear his farewell as he comes in sight of the heavenly sanctuary, where the city shall have no need of the sun, neither of the moon, to shine in it; for the glory of God shall lighten it, and the Lamb shall be the light thereof. And where all who searched the Scriptures with Him and for Him on earth, shall see His face, and His name shall be in their foreheads.

Our Lord and the Sabbath Day

And he said unto them, That the Son of man is Lord
also of the sabbath.

LUKE 6: 5.

THE SABBATH is the subject of constant and painful controversy in the Four Gospels. And therefore it is that I like
so much to leave that controversy and to go back and look
at our Lord as He observed and enjoyed the Sabbath long
before that painful controversy began. Nothing is more
sweet and beautiful to think of than the way the Holy
Child would be "in the spirit" on the Sabbath day from
His earliest childhood up to His perfect manhood. I like to
picture to myself the child Jesus as He read these words for
the first time in the first book of His mother's household
Bible: "Then the heavens and the earth were finished, and
all the host of them. And God blessed the seventh day and
sanctified it: because that in it he had rested from all his
work which God created and made." And then, as the
Holy Child went on to learn the Ten Commandments, He
came on this also: "Remember the Sabbath day to keep it
holy. For in six days the Lord made heaven and earth, the
sea, and all that in them is, and rested the seventh day;
wherefore the Lord blessed the Sabbath day and hallowed
it." And then this commentary on the commandment:
"Wherefore the children of Israel shall keep the Sabbath,
to observe it throughout their generations, for a perpetual
covenant. It is a sign between me and the children of Israel
for ever; for in six days the Lord made heaven and earth,

and on the seventh day he rested, and was refreshed." And then this essence of it: "Ye shall fear every man his mother and his father, and keep my Sabbaths, and reverence my sanctuary; I am the Lord." And so on through all the prophets and psalmists, till He had His heart carried captive with the holy eloquence of the evangelical prophet whose magnificent passages on the sanctification of the Sabbath day not only every devout heart, but every lover of our noblest literature, knows so well. I delight to think of the coming Lord of the Sabbath preparing Himself and being prepared for His future lordship over the Sabbath and over everything else as He found the places where these things were written, and laid them up in His heart and practiced them in His life.

Never and nowhere since the best days of ancient Israel has the Sabbath day been so sanctified and so enjoyed as in our own Church and country of Scotland. The Scottish Sabbath is a proverb from very opposite poles. It is a proverb of the peace and the sweetness and the sanctity and the spiritual fruitfulness of the Christian Sabbath. And, on the other hand, it is to other people a very proverb of gloom and weariness and burdensomeness, and what not. Which of these two poles best speak the truth is best decided by every man's own experience. If my experience is of any interest to any one, here it is. I have had more than sixty years' experience of a scrupulously kept Sabbath day, and all along it has been to me one of my chief blessings in a life full of blessings. I can testify with full honesty and entire integrity that from my childhood I loved the rest and the retirement and the reading and the church and the classes of the Sabbath day with all my heart. I did not know Wordsworth in those early days, but I can truthfully say that he has drawn my exact portrait in his two brothers, Leonard and James. The Sabbath books, few but the best, of those boyhood days of mine, abide with me to this day. And I wish your children and my children no better memories of your home and mine than I have of a good book at my mother's fireside on a Saturday night and a whole Sabbath day. For with us the Sabbath day tidiness and the Sabbath day quiet always began early on Saturday night. Nor did I make Jeremy Taylor's notable acquaintance till long after those early days. But I subscribed to his testimony as soon as I read it: "He who keeps the day most strictly, and most religiously, he keeps it best, and most consonant to the designs of the Church, and the ends of religion, and the opportunity of the present leisure, and the interests of his own soul." Nor did I know William Law till far too long after, but I have never forgotten these weighty words of his on this same subject: "If a man should oblige himself to abstain on the Lord's day from any innocent and lawful things, as traveling, visiting, common conversation, and discoursing upon worldly matters, as trade, news, and the like; if he should devote the day, besides the public worship, to greater retirement, reading, devotion, instruction, and works of charity, it may seem but a small thing or a needless nicety to require a man to abstain from such things as may be done without sin, yet whoever would try the benefit of such a rule would perhaps thereby find such a change made in his spirit, and such a taste of piety raised in his mind, as he was an entire stranger to before." And your own forefathers were wont to rise at six o'clock on the Sabbath morning in this city to hear Edward Irving, our Scottish Hooker, discoursing on this subject in this way: "All letters of business, all messages of business, and all conversation of business, and all books which treat of business, we should exclude. We should not encourage any traffic, nor employ any Sabbath, and grudge not to the people or to myself whatever may refresh and comfort the body or the mind. And if they find that end to be served by walking abroad to meditate and muse upon the works of God, I commend them to that or any other method which they find best for fulfilling the purposes of God. But sure I am, a crowded vehicle, a public inn, a crowded garden, a bustling highway, a park parade, are not the places most fitting for repose and refreshment; and they who so spend the Sabbath, and call it keeping the commandment, do but lie unto the Lord and to their own soul." But among all the Sabbath testimonies of our greatest and best men, there is no testimony that more impresses me and remains more with me, than that of Dr. Johnson. Boswell tells us that Dr. Johnson, in his forty-sixth year, wrote in his Journal this scheme of life for the Lord's day: "Having lived not without an habitual reverence for the Sabbath, yet without that attention to its religious duties which Christianity requires, I resolve henceforth—(1) To rise early, and in order to that, to go to sleep early on Saturday. (2) To use some extraordinary devotion in the morning. (3) To examine the tenor of my life, and particularly the last week; and to mark my advances in religion, or recessions from it. (4) To read the Scriptures methodically with such helps as are at hand. (5) To go to church twice. (6) To read books of divinity, either speculative or practical. (7) To instruct my family. (8) To wear off by meditation any worldly soil contracted in the week."

Now, that, to my mind, is a perfect plan and program of a true Scottish Sabbath. Look well at it.

First: "To rise early, and in order to that, to go to sleep early on Saturday." The Psalms of David are full of early rising on the Sabbath morning. And all up and down the Bible, and all up and down those books of biography and autobiography that come next to the Bible, the same practice is everywhere exhibited and enjoined. And an English writer who was well known to Dr. Johnson must have both rebuked and directed him in this very matter: "I will begin with the last day of the week, and with the latter end of that day, I mean Saturday evening, on which I have fasted ever since I was a youth in Venice, for being delivered from a very great danger. And on Sunday morning I rise earlier than upon other days, to prepare myself for the sanctifying of it."

Second: "To use some extraordinary devotion in the morning." Dr. Johnson's Sabbath day instructor just mentioned, says this also on this subject: "This year I use some extraordinary acts of devotion to usher in the Sunday in hymns and various prayers of my own devising on Saturday night before I go to bed." If any one is at a loss and wishes to be shown an example of an extraordinary act of devotion for a Sabbath morning, I know nothing better than Bishop Andrewes' "First Day of the Week." In his magnificent devotion for the "First Day of the Week" the devout Bishop is carried above himself. Here Andrewes is as good as Hooker is at his seraphic best; this, indeed, is simply Hooker's immortal First Book set to temple music. It is such devotional work as this that justifies the saying that if once you begin to pray with Bishop Andrewes you will continue to pray with him all your days. If you would learn by heart an extraordinary devotion for a Sabbath morning consult the devotional Bishop.

Third: "To examine my advances in religion, or my recessions from it, particularly the last week." To examine in what I have made some real progress last week. In what I have kept a command over myself. When and where I have spoken advisedly with my lips. When and where I held my peace under sore provocation to speak. And when and where I subdued and kept under any other of my besetting sins. As also, when and where I receded, and went back. Against what persons I sinned last week in my anger, in my moroseness, in my envy, in the malice of my heart, and in my evil speaking.

Fourth: "To read the Scriptures methodically with such

helps as are at hand." Who nowadays reads the Scriptures methodically on the Lord's day, or on any other day? Is there any other book in the whole world that is read so immethodically as the Scriptures? Any history, any biography, any philosophy, any poem, any novel? No, not one. Most men read the Bible just where it chances to open, and it is a bare chance if it opens some days at all. And yet what a divine opportunity it is to read the Book of all books methodically, if only we had Dr. Johnson's noble mind about method in the Bible and on the Sabbath day. "And with such helps as are at hand." Only, we must ourselves secure that the right helps in this matter are indeed at hand. The right helps will not come to our hand of their own accord. When you want to have any real help of any kind at hand for any purpose, if you do not already possess it, you go to where it is sold and buy it, and you bring it home and put it in a place set apart for it, so that you may be able to lay your hand on it the moment you need it. And if you are not able to buy it, you borrow it, or you beg it, as Dr. Johnson first borrowed and then begged *The Appeal to All Who Doubt,* from Miss Boothby. "I return you Law's *Appeal,* which, however, I entreat you to give me. Samuel Johnson, *impransus."*

Fifth: "To instruct my family." I wish he had taken time to tell us how he did it, and how he succeeded in it. For many of us who are quite good hands at instructing other men's families are but poor hands at instructing our own. For my part, I think that just to make Dr. Johnson's Sabbath-day resolutions, and not to recede from them, is the very best way of instructing both ourselves and our families. For it is a true proverb that example is much better than precept. To rise early on Sabbath morning, as Dr. Johnson did, and then to fill up the whole day as he did— that will impress and instruct your family as nothing else will. To select an interesting Sabbath book also, and to read it, a page each all round, is a tried and a sure way of instructing a Sabbath-day family. To give each member of your family a copy of the *Pilgrim's Progress,* for instance, and the poorest father in the land can do that; and then to read all round a page each; and then to copy each into his own neat little notebook the happy expressions, and the striking names of the people and the places you have met with in your home reading, and then to index them all carefully—for my family and for myself I have never discovered any more delightful way of spending a Sabbath hour than in something like that. As also to study so as to make the family worship as interesting and instructive as the wit of man can make it; as also the catechism and the hymnbook —what might we not overtake in our families in fifty-two such days of more or less leisure and opportunity! "Father, is this a good book for Sabbath?" "Judge for yourself. Six days shalt thou read Greek, and Latin, and history, and travels, and stories. But the Sabbath is the Sabbath, and it has its own special and proper books. Think for yourself who is the Lord of the Sabbath day, and what He has made the Sabbath day for, and then decide for yourself what books are proper and becoming for you to read on His day and under His eye."

And lastly: "To wear off by meditation any worldly soil contracted in the week." If you are like me you will need something much more pungent than mere meditation to do that. At the same time, much concentrated and uninterrupted meditation is absolutely necessary to begin with. And, among its many other priceless blessings, the Scottish Sabbath has always been cherished and loved for the opportunity and for the assistance it gives to true meditation, and to the washing away of worldly soil, and all other kinds of soil. And a favorite Scottish psalm expresses that purifying operation to perfection:

Do thou with hyssop sprinkle me,
  I shall be cleansed so;
Yea, wash Thou me, and then I shall
  Be whiter than the snow.

Thy Daily Cross

*And he said to them all, If any man will come after me,
let him deny himself, and take up his cross daily, and
follow me.*

LUKE 9: 23.

SUPPORTED and directed and encouraged by these words
of our Lord, let us look somewhat closely at some of the
crosses that we all lay every day on one another. For, over
and above those crosses that come to us immediately and
directly from the hand of God, there are many other crosses
that we all lay continually on one another. There are things
in all our lives that chafe and fret and crucify our hearts
continually, and that is so partly because of the persons who
are the causes of those crosses, and partly because we have
not as yet taken the right way to deal with those persons
and with those crosses that they lay on us. Being what we
are, how could it be but that we should in many ways become great crosses to one another? To take a number of
selfish human beings, and to set them down in the closest
relationships with one another, and that sometimes for a
long lifetime—the wonder is, not that there are so many
crosses among us, but that there are so few catastrophes.

Even in the happiest and the most harmonious of homes
the parent will sometimes be a very heavy cross to the child,
and sometimes the child to the parent, and sometimes the
wife to the husband, and sometimes the husband to the wife.
Those you love best may be the cause of a constant and an
acute cross to you. To take a common case, a solicitous fa-

218

ther will sometimes see his son forming the closest attachments to people of whom he cannot possibly approve. He will see his growing son gradually falling off from the friendships of his father's house and forming his most intimate friendships among men whose opinions in religion and whose habits and practices in morals and in manners all combine to constitute a cross too heavy for his father to bear. A simple difference in church connection will sometimes be a very sharp cross to some fathers. A boy who has been brought up to be a Presbyterian, to be a son of the Reformers and the Covenanters, and who has turned his back on his father's faith, and has become, say, an Episcopalian—there are fathers so narrow and so weak and so self-willed as to make that a lifelong cross to themselves and to their households. Or, again, their sons from being at one time true and evangelical believers have, in the jargon of the day, become agnostics, or again, absolute skeptics, till their heart-crossed fathers have been heard to say that they would sooner have seen their sons in their grave. A difference in politics also will do it. A different taste in literature or in art or in anything else whatsoever will do it, if the difference is persistently brought up, and is persistently argued over at home. Again, irregular hours, and other bad habits at home will do it. And so on, till crosses, the smallest and the slightest to begin with, will grow to be the most galling and heart-crushing of crosses to a father's and a mother's heart.

Then, again, out of doors, and in your business life, there are men with whom you are compelled to stand in the closest of business relationships, men whose tempers, and whose manners, and whose whole treatment of you, continually exasperate you. There are men whose talents and whose successes are a constant temptation and a constant cross to you, and yet you cannot get away from their immediate neighborhood. And then over against that, there are men whose lack of talent and whose consequent lack of success are to be a lifelong hindrance and impoverishment to you. In a thousand such ways as these some men's lives seem to them to be laid out, both at home and abroad, to make them the most cross-bearing and the most continually crucified men in all the world, till sometimes they feel as if they were simply bleeding to death through causes and in ways of which no human being has any conception, or ever will have any conception.

Now, though no mortal man may ever guess that you are fast sinking into your grave under the weight of such crosses as these, it is no guess with God. He knows all about it, and the Son of God knows all about it. And thus it is that He is having this text of His applied so closely to your special case: "Then he said to them all, If any man will come after me, let him deny himself, and take up his cross daily, and follow me." "Let him take up his cross daily." Now, with what point and power that word "daily" will come home to some men among us! Some others, no doubt, will set down that strong word as just another of our Lord's staggering hyperboles, as just another of His almost too strong statements. But there are those among us who see and feel in this scripture that their Divine Lord knows all about their deepest and most secret cross, and that He speaks home to their broken heart when He recognizes that theirs is a daily cross. For so it is. As for them, their daily cross is back on their hearts every morning before their eyes are open. They carry their cross about with them all the day, and it lies down beside them every night as their inseparable and lifelong bedfellow.

And bear your cross believingly as well as daily. That is to say, though your daily cross seems to you to come exclusively and wholly from the hands of such and such a person beside you, aye, and even though your daily cross does demonstrably come to you from the hands of that person, at the same time take it up daily and bear it daily, believing that at bottom and far out of your sight God's hand is absolutely alone in laying your cross on you. "Is there evil in the city, and the Lord hath not done it?" And is there a heavy cross on any human heart, and is not the hand of God alone at the bottom of it? Believe therefore that the watchfulness of God and the wisdom of God and the love of God are all ultimately and exclusively at the bottom of your cross also. Every day you see with your eyes the people who lay your cross on you, and you do not as yet with your eyes see God. But be you sure He is not far away. For dear in God's sight is the cross of His saints. Believe that, and be sure that what you see not now as to the true author and the true nature and the true intention of your cross, you shall hereafter see all that as clear as day, and that before very long. Every new morning, then, take up your cross from the very hand of God Himself, and carry it all day in His strength, and under His all-seeing and His all-sympathizing eye.

No one has ever understood crosses better or has written better about crosses than Samuel Rutherford, and that was because he had so many of his own and bore them so believingly and so bravely. And in one of his best letters he says to Lady Kenmure that as for his Aberdeen cross it is "full of talk" to him in his imprisonment. His cross is full, he says, of the most moving eloquence to him. Some whole days and some whole nights his cross speaks to him so loudly and so unceasingly that he can hear nothing else. "I am come from thy God, to thee, O minister of Anwoth," says his cross to him. "And I have a great blessing from thy God to thee hidden under my black and coarse cloak." And sometimes, when Rutherford forgot himself and began to complain to God and to man about his cross, it would say this to him: "Look well, Samuel Rutherford, at that cross of your neighbor so-and-so. And say, would you exchange crosses with him?" Also when he was particularly rebellious his cross would look him sternly in the face, and would rebuke him and upbraid him in this way: "Samuel Rutherford! Hast thou wholly forgotten the sins of thy youth? Think, sir, what thy cross might well have been, aye, and at one time almost was! Had God dealt with thee after thy sins, thou wouldst not have been writing consolatory letters to God's afflicted saints in Scotland today. My man! had God dealt with thee as He has dealt with some of thy class fellows, thou wouldst long before now have been in thine own place." All that, and much more like that, Rutherford's Aberdeen cross said to him without ceasing, till he became our greatest authority on crosses in all sacred literature.

Take up your cross, then, both daily and believingly. And all the time be sure to exercise your imagination on your cross and on all the circumstances thereof. For one thing, imagine yourself in your offensive neighbor's place. Put yourself inside the mind and inside the heart and inside the history and inside all the circumstances of the man who is such a cross to you. For, depend on it, we are all as great crosses to other people as they are to us. Not seldom, when we are tossing on our bed with pain and with rage and with rebellion, the very person we are accusing and cursing before God is at that same moment, and just through the wall, wrestling with God either to cut his life short or ours, because he can endure us no longer. Now, to imagine that and to believe that is true wisdom. To imagine that and to believe that will make you humble and contrite and patient and kind and forgiving. He is a hopeless fool who goes on all his life thinking and saying and praying that he is the only injured man and the only insulted man and the only despised man and the only cross-bearing man in all the household, in all the congregation, and in all the community. Yes, we should think we overhear all our neighbor's complaints and prayers to God about ourselves.

And then there is this: it is quite possible that it may be the very best thing about you that makes you such a cross to some other man. And if that is your case just imagine yourself back in that house in which Jesus of Nazareth was born and brought up. Jesus Christ composed this text for you out of His own experience. For He was a constant cross to His brothers and His sisters at home, and He knew it and He bowed His head and accepted it. First, His doctrine, and then His manner of life, made them all miserable at home. I will not say that they made Him miserable in return, but they often made Him very sad. For by their cruel treatment of His doctrine and of Himself they laid a far heavier cross on His broken heart than ever Pilate laid on His bleeding back. Return in imagination to all that and it will help to make you more humble and more meek and more considerate and more patient, till at last you are made absolutely like your Lord.

And all that will end in enabling you to bear your cross silently and uncomplainingly. Many a cross that is laden with spiritual blessings of the best kind is completely frustrated, and leaves nothing but uncompensated pain behind it, because the cross-bearer would not hold his peace about his cross. And, indeed, you will need superhuman strength and self-command to enable you just to hold your rebellious tongue about what you are suffering. You will feel sometimes that you could bear your cross far better if you could but once break out and make those who are your daily cross to know what you think about them. But on no account ever yield to that temptation. That thought is not of God, it is of the devil. Your outburst about your cross would not remove your cross from you. Far from that. Your heavy cross would be tenfold heavier after your outburst and you would be ten times weaker to bear it.

> Prune thou thy words, the thoughts control
> That o'er thee swell and throng;
> They will condense within thy soul
> And change to purpose strong.

And not only do not speak to any one about your cross, but to the end of your life hide your cross from every human eye. Do not let any one so much as guess that you have a cross. Do not be sour or sullen or ostentatiously unhappy over your cross. Do not sigh over it so as to attract attention to it and to win sympathy to yourself. Be all the more sweet and genial to all men all the time your heart is breaking. Wash your face and anoint your head till no one will believe that anything of the nature of a cross had ever come within a hundred miles of you. And then you will sometimes have this to think about so as to help you to keep silence. Halyburton says that sometimes he would see his former sin clearly written all over his present punishment. And so will you see your sin in your cross till you will say with the St. Andrews professor, and with another great cross-bearer: Why should a man like me complain? It is good for a man like me that he bear his cross for his sin. He sitteth alone and keepeth silence, because the secret of the Lord is with him; and because he cannot speak about that secret to anyone but to the Lord Himself. He putteth his mouth in the dust, if so there be any hope.

I have claimed for Samuel Rutherford the foremost place among all the authorities on crosses and cross-bearing. And in closing I will give you his most classical passage on this whole subject: "If you take up your cross handsomely, and frankly, and, above all, believingly, your heaviest cross will become such a burden to you as its wings are to a bird and as its sails are to a ship." Now, poetical and paradoxical and rhetorical as that sounds at first, it is all the time literally and demonstrably true. What would you say from today to try that way with your cross? Just make your own experiment on that way and see for yourself. You have tried many other ways with your cross; perhaps you have not as yet tried Rutherford's way. You have tried a life of complaint and remonstrance against God and man. You have tried bitter words and still more bitter thoughts against the man who has laid your cross on you. You have retaliated on him again and again, both by words and by deeds. You have even gone to Gethsemane, and have again and again fallen down in a sweat of blood before God, that He would take away your cross from you. But there it is, heavier and more galling and more sickening and more murderous to your soul than ever. Yes, you have prayed and prayed about your cross till you are wearied to death with unanswered prayer. Try Rutherford's plan. On the barest chance that he is right you might try his plan before you kill yourself. Take up your cross handsomely then. Take it up silently. Take it up believingly. And give that way of it a good trial. Try it for a week, try it for a month, and if you are spared so long try it for a year. And I will take it on me to tell you what you will then say. You will say that, after a long and persevering trial of Rutherford's way of it, for your part, you subscribe with all your heart to this in Isaiah his fortieth chapter: "Why sayest thou, O Jacob, and speakest, O Israel, My way is hid from the Lord, and my judgment is passed over from my God? For he giveth power to the faint; and to them that have no might he increaseth strength. Even the youths shall faint and be weary, and the young men shall utterly fall: but they that wait upon the Lord shall renew their strength; they shall mount up with wings as eagles; they shall run, and not be weary; and they shall walk, and not faint."

And that will be your daily doxology till all your crosses are laid in your grave to see no resurrection.

The Shorter Catechism

QUESTION 38: *What benefits do believers receive from Christ at the resurrection?*

ANSWER: *At the resurrection, believers being raised up in glory,[1] shall be openly acknowledged and acquitted in the day of judgment,[2] and made perfectly blessed in the full enjoying of God to all eternity.[3]*

A_t *the resurrection,* . . . The resurrection of the dead is exclusively a doctrine of the Word of God. It nowhere appears in the religions of paganism. That the soul should continue to live after death was the faith and hope of many of the best men in heathendom; but that there should be a resurrection of the body, and a reunion of soul and body forever, this is a doctrine derived wholly from the Word of God. The Athenians in Paul's day believed in the existence of God. They raised no opposition even when Paul preached the unity, spirituality, providence, and fatherhood of God; but when he went on from these things to preach

[1] I Cor. 15: 43: "It is raised in glory . . ."
[2] Matt. 25: 23: "Well done, good and faithful servant; thou hast been faithful over a few things, I will make thee ruler over many things: enter thou into the joy of thy lord." Matt. 10: 32: "Whosoever therefore shall confess me before men, him will I confess also before my Father which is in heaven."
[3] I John 3: 2: "Beloved, now are we the sons of God; and it doth not yet appear what we shall be: but we know that, when he shall appear, we shall be like him; for we shall see him as he is." I Cor. 13: 12: "For now we see through a glass, darkly; but then face to face: now I know in part; but then shall I know even as also I am known." I Thess. 4: 17: ". . . so shall we ever be with the Lord."

Jesus and the resurrection, that was a "new doctrine" to them, and some mocked, though others said, "We will hear thee again of this matter."

There is nothing taught in the text touching the resurrection of unbelievers, because the Catechism is engaged in tracing the benefits that "believers" receive from Christ; and though all the dead shall rise again, not all shall "attain to the resurrection" set forth in the text.

believers being raised up in glory, . . . This is the last time "believers" shall bear that name. From the day of their effectual calling to the day of their resurrection they have been "believers," but after their resurrection there is no more room for faith; then and thereafter they shall know even as they are known. At the resurrection Christ shall change their vile body, that it may be fashioned like unto His glorious body. But what that glory shall consist in we cannot in this life tell; we are "believers" in the resurrection and the resurrection life. "Therefore some of our divines say that our Saviour Christ did not simply merit the resurrection of the dead, for that apart from Him they must have risen again and been brought to judgment: but these glorious qualifications the saints have at the resurrection, which is the preparation to the glory in heaven—these He merited, this some divines say" (Goodwin).

shall be openly acknowledged and acquitted in the day of judgment, . . . God had *secretly* acknowledged and acquitted them on the day of their first justification. But both their faith in Christ and their acceptance before God had been hidden with Christ in God. The whole transaction of their renewal, union to Christ, pardon, and acceptance was unknown to the world in which they dwelt; in many cases true believers themselves had never come to a clear assurance that they possessed these saving benefits. But all that will then be made manifest both to themselves and to all men. What had been spoken in secret shall then be told from the housetops.

"Christ hath not all His members up to Him, nor are they out of all danger, as I may so express it; for though at the day of judgment to the saints there is no real danger, yet they are to give an account of their actions, and there remaineth a final sentence to be pronounced upon them by the Great Judge, and in that sense there is a forgiveness of sins then; therefore Paul prayeth that he may find mercy at that day" (Goodwin).

> Jesus, Thy blood and righteousness
> My beauty are, my glorious dress:
> 'Midst flaming worlds in these arrayed,
> With joy shall I lift up my head.
>
> Bold shall I stand in that great day:
> For who aught to my charge shall lay?
> Fully, through these, absolved I am
> From sin and fear, from guilt and shame.

and be made perfectly blessed . . .

> It may not be
> That one, who looks upon that light can turn
> To other objects, willingly, his view.
> For all the good that will may covet, there
> Is summ'd: and all, elsewhere defective found,
> Complete.—*Paradise*. (See the whole canto, 33.)

See also the talk that the Shining Ones held with the pilgrims about the glory of the place.

in the full enjoying of God . . . "But especially in the immediate vision and fruition of God the Father, of our Lord Jesus Christ, and of the Holy Spirit, to all eternity" (Larger Catechism). "To sit down with Abraham, Isaac, and Jacob was the phraseology of the Old Testament, but

to sit down with us—with Father, Son, and Holy Ghost—
this is Christ's language, this is New Testament language"
(Goodwin).

"Man's chief end" is now attained. (See Question 1.) The
Scriptures constantly teach that man's only true happiness
is in God, and that his full happiness in God cannot be attained in this life, but that believing men have that happiness assured to them in the life to come. Commenting on
John 14: 6, Godet says: "Jesus here substitutes the Father
for the Father's house. For it is not in heaven that we are
to find God, but in God that we are to find heaven."

to all eternity. "When time and sin together cease." Both
a prophet and an apostle join in teaching us that eye hath
not seen, nor ear heard, nor man's heart conceived, what
God has prepared for those that love Him. When the
bodies of the just rise at the general resurrection, with
their senses spiritualized and rendered capable of pleasures
which do not fall within their province now, and with perhaps many new senses developed in the immortal body
which were unknown in its mortal days, the pure pleasures
of their glorified senses must be something quite beyond
the power of our imagination to picture to itself" (Faber).

Uses.—1. "As Christ would have us to be certainly persuaded that there shall be a day of judgment, both to de-
   ter all men from sin, and for the greater consolation of
   the godly in their adversity; so will He have that day
   unknown to men, that they may shake off all carnal se-
   curity, and be always watchful, because they know not
   at what hour the Lord will come: and may be ever prepared to say, Come, Lord Jesus, come quickly. Amen"
   (Confession).
2. Luther warns us: "The flesh ever seeks to be glorified
   before it is crucified: exalted before it is abased."
3. It is often ignorantly and frivolously charged against

Christian men that it is selfish in them to seek heaven and glory for their own souls; but no man who is truly seeking salvation will be moved by that accusation. When men really begin to seek their salvation, and to turn their faces to the glory of heaven, then it is that all selfish and ignoble desires receive their death blow. It is not selfish, surely, for the diseased to seek healing, or the hungry food, or the prodigal his father's house. So far from this being a sign that the heart is selfish, there is no surer sign that it is being sanctified.

4. "Pliable. The hearing of all this is enough to ravish one's heart; but are these things to be enjoyed? How shall we get to be sharers hereof?

"Christian. The Lord, the Governor of the country, hath recorded that in this book; the substance of which is, If we be truly willing to have it, He will bestow it upon us freely." [1]

QUESTIONS

1. Give New Testament passages where the Resurrection life is called a Regeneration, a Redemption, and a Restitution, and explain these terms when so applied.

2. Reconcile "acquitted" in the text with the teaching of Answer 33.

[1] *Pilgrim's Progress.*

The Melancholy Temperament

I<small>T HAS LONG BEEN</small> a popular proverb that certain temperaments obtain and prevail among certain races and nations of men. Our old literature is full of the sanguineness, light-mindedness, overconfidence, and inconstancy of France; the phlegm, solidity, steadiness, and endurance of Germany; the brag and the hot breath of Spain; the quick choler—a word and a blow—of Italy; and the melancholy of England, where men take their very pleasures sadly. "A peculiar vein of constitutional sadness belongs to the Greek temperament," says Professor Butcher in his fine paper on the melancholy of the Greeks, in which its learned author traces the manifestations of that melancholy down through the whole of the Greek classics. Not that all Frenchmen are light-minded, or all Germans steady and enduring, or all Spaniards, or all Italians, choleric; or all Englishmen, or all Greeks, melancholy. But, broadly speaking, the statement is true. It may be in their race and lineage; it may be in their religious, political, or social conditions; or it may be in all these things taken together; but there is unquestionably a prevailing temperament in all these, and in all the other distinct races and nations of men. Then, again, it has been held that certain occupations, certain pursuits, certain interests, certain professions, and certain handicrafts even, tend to produce, develop, and perpetuate certain temperaments and certain dispositions, and there is a good deal to be said for that doctrine also.

Dr. Butcher quotes Aristotle approvingly as saying that

all men of genius are of a melancholy temperament. And that, when it is said by one of the profoundest students of human nature the world has ever seen, is all but final. For, besides being a man of a supreme genius himself, Aristotle lived among a people, and in an age, in which genius blossomed out as never before or since on the face of the earth. And all that is wanting to make his affirmation absolutely final and conclusive is the observation and experience of like observers and like experimenters in the ages, and among the races of men, since his day. And though there have undoubtedly been men of genius who were of a light, gay, elastic, and vivacious temperament, yet by far the greatest, the most original, and the most commanding men, in all ages, go to prove the author of the *Ethics* to have been, not only a profound psychologist and moralist in his own day, but a true prophet for all the days and all the races that have come after him.

"A more than ordinary depth of thought," says Jacob Behmen, "produces this temperament." There you have the whole truth and the best truth in a nutshell. Let a more than ordinary depth of thought be found in any man, and that man's mind will naturally and necessarily move among the mysteries, the solemnities, the sadnesses, and the awful issues of human life, till, as sure as shadow follows substance, that man is a melancholy man. And thus it is that when, either in life or in literature, you meet with a man of an extraordinary depth of thought, you will see shafts of sadness and chasms of melancholy sinking down into that man's mind and heart and character—clefts and chasms that will offend, exasperate, and scare away all light-minded and shallow-hearted onlookers.

Great examples, in a great subject like this, are far better than any man's disquisitions and argumentations on it. For great examples are the disquisitions and the argumentations of God. Take two great examples on this matter then. And, first, take that of the author of *The Four Complexions* and *The Divine Vision*: "Before I was led into the light of God, I saw, and thought, and felt like the men around me. But when I was awakened, and went on, I fell into a great melancholy. Brooding on the darkness of this world—the height of the heavens and the depth of the earth—men, good men on the one hand and bad men on the other—chance, fate, providence—the whole unfathomable mystery of life, I became very dejected, melancholy, and mournful, and could find no consolation, not even in Holy Writ. The deeper my thoughts went, the deeper did my spirit fill with sadness, till, after long and sore wrestling, I got light upon many things which had been before that as dark as midnight to me." But this deep thinker's speculative, philosophical, and theological melancholy only prepared the way for a spiritual and an experimental melancholy which took deeper and deeper possession of his mind and heart, till that light broke on his melancholy mind and heart in which there is no shadow, and which never sets.

John Foster was a man of an extraordinary depth of thought, and this is how he writes to one of his most thoughtful correspondents: "Everything that interests my heart leads me into this mingled emotion of melancholy and the sublime. I have lost all taste for the light and the gay; rather, I never had any such taste. I turn disgusted and contemptuous from insipid and shallow folly, to lave in the tide, the stream, of deeper sentiments. I have criminally neglected regular, studious thinking for many years. My greatest defects are in regard to religion, on which subject, as it respects myself, I want to have a profound and solemn investigation, which I foresee must be mingled with a great deal of painful and repentant feeling. What a serious task it is to confront one's self with faithful truth, and to see one's self by a light that will not flatter! At the last tribunal no one will regret having been a habitual and rigorous judge of self." Does any one ask what a true and a wise "melancholy" is? Does any one wish to know what that mourning is which our Lord pronounces to be blessed? I know no better English example of it than John Foster; I know no better German example of it than Jacob Behmen, and no better example of it ever lived than the French Blaise Pascal. Dante, Cromwell, Johnson, and Cowper will occur to all in this connection. And the melancholy of all these men is a melancholy worthy of the solemn name. Their melancholy is that into which all truly great minds, and all truly deep, awakened, and enlightened hearts, more and more sink down, till they and their melancholy are all swallowed up in the ocean of light and liberty that is at God's right hand.

All those masters in the intellectual and spiritual life both lived and wrote in a profound melancholy; and "melancholy," says Samuel Rutherford, a master also, "is such a complexion that, when it is sanctified, it becomes a seat of mortification and of humble walking." Yes, let the melancholy temperament only be sanctified; let the darkness, and the doubt, and the gloom, and the despondency, and the querulousness, and the moroseness, be all taken out of it, and you will straightway have all that depth, and strength, and detachment, and superiority, and sovereignty of mind and heart, which Rutherford calls the mortification and the sanctification of the saints. And, as he says, it will be a seat of humble walking also. For the truly humble man—who is he but the man who has gone down deep into himself, and who abides there, and walks with God there? No man can continue to be a proud man who walks much with God in his own heart. No man carries his head high there. No man looks down on his neighbor there. He may be the most intellectual of men; he may be the most spiritual of men; and if only he is both, then you have the humblest man that ever was on this side heaven. If John Milton's melancholy is the daughter of retirement and learning, then, by the Spirit of God, she is afterwards the sure mother of humility and mortification, and thus of all the fruits of the Spirit.

But sanguine, choleric, phlegmatic, melancholy, and all— we all belong to the same family of the Fall. God has made us all of the same blood. And we all have our own portion and plot of human nature selected, allotted, and laid out for us to till, and to keep, and to reap for God. Some men's plots are harder to make much of than others'. Some men's plots are already full of stones, and weeds, and fallen fences, through past generations of misuse and neglect. One man's vineyard will lie more to the sun than his neighbor's; but every man's inheritance summons him to his utmost skill, and care, and labor. With that, the most unpromising piece of ground will bring forth an honest harvest, and without that the best ground that ever was laid out will soon run into a wilderness.

We cannot all have the same temperament. One will have a better and a more easily handled temperament than his neighbor. But the best temperament has its dangers, and the worst is not without its compensations and opportunities. And a wise man will give all his attention to himself, and will hail all offered help to know himself, and to make the best of himself. To climb up and look over the wall and call the attention of the passer-by to the weeds in his neighbor's garden—no wise man will do that. No man but a fool will do that. His own hoe and his own mattock will take up all his time and all his strength. No wise man will attend to anything in this world so much as to his own heart, and to his temperament and his circumstances as they affect his heart. Are you, then, a man of a melancholy temperament? Is your constant temptation to gloom, and sadness, and moroseness, and peevishness? Do clouds, and fogs, and sour east winds hang continually over your soul? Do you spend all your days in "the melancholy inn"? And would you escape all that? Or, if all that cannot be escaped in this life, how are you best to do? You will be careful to read how all the great melancholiacs did. You will study and imitate the great men, and especially the great saints, of your own temperament. You will make a little library of the melancholy men of God. You will worm into their secrets. You will work yourself into their ways. And, as you sit alone, and read their psalms and their prayers and their diaries and their letters and their confidential conversations, you will ever and anon lift up your imagination and your heart to that life on which they have now all entered, to that city where there is no night, and no sea, and where God has wiped all tears from their eyes.

"Now I saw in my dream that Christiana thought she heard in a grove, a little way off on the right hand, a most curious melodious note, with words much like these:

> Goodness and mercy all my life
>   Shall surely follow me;
> And in God's house for evermore
>   My dwelling-place shall be.

"So she asked Prudence what 'twas that made those curious notes? They are, said she, our country birds: they sing these notes but seldom except it be at the spring, when the flowers appear, and the sun shines warm, and then you may hear them all day long. I often, said she, go out to hear them; we also ofttimes keep them tame in our house. They are very fine company for us when we are melancholy;

also they make the woods, and groves, and solitary places, places desirous to be in.

> "His truth at all times firmly stood,
>
> —that melodious note went on in the wood—
>
> And shall from age to age endure."

The Sanguine Temperament

From the very earliest days of the medical and mental sciences the bodily constitutions of men, especially as those bodily constitutions bear on the mind, have been called the complexions and the temperaments. And the outstanding and distinctive temperaments have been classified and designated from the earliest days as the sanguine temperament, the choleric temperament, the phlegmatic temperament, and the melancholy temperament. Not that any man was ever made up of blood and of blood alone, or of choler alone, or of phlegm alone, or of black bile alone. The four temperaments, as they are found in actual and living men, have undergone as many combinations and permutations as there have been individual men and women on the face of the earth. At the same time, some one of the four great temperaments has predominated and has had the upper hand in the construction and constitution of every man. And thus it is that, broadly speaking, each one among us may quite correctly be described as a sanguine man, or a choleric man, or a phlegmatic man, or a melancholy man, according as this or that temperament or complexion has the ruling hand over him.

> So in every body,
> The choler, melancholy, phlegm, and blood,
> By reason that they flow continually
> In some one part, and are not continent,
> Receive the name of humors. Now, thus far
> It may, by metaphor, apply itself
> Unto the general disposition:

> As when some one peculiar quality
> Doth so possess a man, that it doth draw
> All his effects, his spirits, and his powers,
> In their confluctions, all to run one way,
> This may be truly said to be a humor.

"The blood is the life." And a sanguine temperament is just good old medical Latin for a body and a mind full of blood—a body so full of blood, indeed, that the blood runs over and fills the mind also. A sanguine man, then, is a man whose blood is his staple and chief feature; and that not of his body only, but much more of his mind and his heart. The sanguine man's whole mental and moral life, his whole intellectual character and spiritual complexion, takes the tinge and the temperature of his blood. His blood builds up his body, and fills his body full of all its members and all their operations. And so is it with his mind. It is the bounding tide of blood in the hearts of our young men that keeps this otherwise old and withered world always warm and full of hope and joy. The angel of youth with his purple wings descends on this stagnant pool, in the porches of which a great multitude of impotent folk lie; and, as he alights, health and love and hope and joy are spread all round him. Thus it is that while there is always a generation of halt and withered waiting for death, there is always a new race rising up with thankful and hopeful hearts. And it is their blood that does it. It is their young blood that does it. It is their sanguine temperament that does it. If it were for nothing else but that it keeps bright eyes, and ruddy cheeks, and clapping hands, and dancing feet alive on this place of graves, how much we should owe to both the youthful blood of the body and the youthful blood of the soul.

The onward march of mankind also, the ever-advancing providences of the Living God, the expansion and the extension of the nations of the earth, as well as the spread and the fullness of the Church of Christ—all these are simply bound up with the sanguine temperament. For that happy temperament is open, hopeful, believing, enterprising, and responsive to all that is true and good. The sanguine temperament beareth all things, believeth all things, hopeth all things, endureth all things. So truly good is this temperament in a man, and so useless and so evil does that man become who is devoid of it, that, when it dulls down, decays, and dies out in any man, we may as well bury that man out of our sight at once. His day is past. His work is done. Gather him to his fathers, and let his sons take up his once living name, and bear it onward into the new worlds of God and of man that are ever opening their great gates to all open-minded and open-hearted men.

All down human history, both sacred and profane, we see the great deliverances, the great advancements, the great conquests and attainments, the great enlargements and the great enrichments that this so generous temperament of the heart of man has achieved. Look at all the true leaders of men in all ages. Look at the pioneers and those who have prepared the way. Look at the men who opened their eyes, opened their hearts, spoke the first word, and took the first step. Look at home also. Who is the life of your house at home? Who is your staff? Who is the wine of your life? Is it not that son or that daughter who has a heart, and a mind, and an eye, and an ear, and a hand, and a foot, and warm and bounding blood in them all?

And yet, with all that, it must be confessed, it is with a certain "tinge of disapprobation" that we usually speak of the sanguine temperament. Now, why is that?

With so much to be said in behalf of this temperament, why is it that there undoubtedly is a certain tincture of disapprobation and depreciation in this epithet? "Ye sanguine, shallow-hearted boys!" exclaims the master of insight and of expression. As much as to say that the sanguine in this world are the young. They are boys rather than men. As also that great depth and great endurance of heart do not usually reside with great warmth and fullness of heart. "The man of a purely sanguine temperament," says a medical writer, "his blood soon boils and soon cools; his heart rules his head; action precedes thought. It is a word and a blow, and then great sorrow for it. I know two partners in business," he continues, "one sanguine, the other bilious. The bilious has often to throw cold water on the projects of the sanguine, who almost invariably fires up and says too much, and then he is miserable and ready to allow and to yield up anything. Inconstancy and levity," he adds, "are the chief attributes of the men of this temperament; they are good, generous, full of feeling, quick, impassioned, but fickle. Excessive and constant variety is to them as much a necessity as an enjoyment." That is much too strong; but, at the same time, there is some truth in it. There is just enough truth in it to justify the scornful and contemptuous exclamation in the play, "Ye younglings! ye sanguine, shallow-hearted boys!"

From the very fact that we usually associate the sanguine temperament with youth, there is more than a tinge of disapprobation and blame when we so describe a grown-up man. He is a sanguine man, we say. We do not, in as many words, say that he is still a child; but, at bottom, that is what we mean.

When we say that a grown-up man is a sanguine man, we really mean to convey to you that he is still a boy, or, at the most, a very young man. We intend to hint that he has not really lived in the world of grown-up men at all. He has not learned his lesson in the sobering school of life. He has not yet laid to heart the defeats, the disappointments, the arrests, the overthrows, the crooks, and the crosses of human life. He is still in his salad days, and green in judgment. He is still a sanguine-hearted boy, when, by this time, he should have been a sober-minded and a serious-hearted man.

We see the misleading and mischief-making side of the sanguine temperament in the way that many men take up, and run away with, this and that new thing. Good things, useful things, needful and necessary things are taken up, run away with, put out of their proper places and proportions, and are greatly hindered and injured by men of an oversanguine, impulsive, and enthusiastic temperament. We see political, social, ecclesiastical, religious, and many other schemes, plans, and programs that every day are being taken up, and for a time run to death, by the oversanguine and the inexperienced. They are all good things in their places; they are all needful and necessary things; but they are all injured past repair when they get into the hot hands of the men who think about, talk about, and will let you think about, and talk about, nothing else. Those are the men who set out to wash the Ethiopian white with rose water, to bind Samson with green grass, and to tame a leopard with a child's toy.

The mischiefs of this temperament, when it enters into religious life, we see all around us every day. The victims of the sanguine temperament are always discovering some new thing in their religion—a new minister, a new evangelist, a new doctrine, and a short cut to salvation. Like Pliable, they cannot get you to go fast enough for them. Lo here! or Lo there! they are continually crying. But a short time comes and goes, and another new thing is discovered, another new nostrum, another new man. Want of depth, want of real seriousness, want of steadfastness, want of endurance, want of a lasting loyalty to any man, or to any cause—these things have brought, not a tinge of disapprobation only, but a positive contempt and scorn on the oversanguine temperament, and especially on that temperament in the most serious of all things—the soul of man and the salvation of God.

At the close of his *Treatise of the Four Complexions,* Teutonicus says some things like this to those of his readers who are of this complexion. Thy complexion, he says, is a right noble complexion; and in it thou mayest live a right orderly, calm, sober, and most useful life, if only thou art on the watch over it, and over thyself in it. There is a certain scope, horizon, and atmosphere in thy peculiar complexion; and thus by means of it thou art capable of great undertakings and great attainments. Thou art happily open to what is new; look well to thyself, and keep true to that good thing when it is old and no longer new. Thou art much inclined to love; place thy love on its right object; give thy whole heart to it, and be faithful to it till death. This cold world will often gibe at thee for the warmth of thy heart. But a little passing scorn will afterwards bring thee the more honor before God and man, and both in this world and in the world to come.

The Choleric Temperament

FROM THE very earliest days choler has been the universally accepted and well-understood name of that lymph, rheum, or humor of the body which was supposed to cause heat in the mind and irascibility in the temper. "If any man's soul," says Behmen, "be clothed about with the choleric complexion, then he is tempted to be a fiery, fierce, fretful, and wrathful man. These things rise up in the choleric man's soul, anger, pride, ambition, and desire of exaltation. A wish to tread all other men under his feet, a disposition to despise and insult the poor and miserable, tyranny and murder—these are in the heart of every choleric man. The devil does not much need to tempt this temperament; he has but to pipe, and the choleric man rises up and dances to his music."

But let us begin with the good side of our somewhat suspicious subject. For God has made all things good in their proper place and at their proper season; and bile, both black and yellow, among the rest—bile in the body and choler in the mind. This is the fiery temperament. But, then, fire also is good, for was not fire the gift of Heaven at the first? Fire is a bad master indeed, but it is one of the very best of servants. And so is anger, which is just the fire of the soul. In his eighth sermon, Bishop Butler institutes a characteristic inquiry into anger. That profound sermon contains at once an inquiry, an exposition, a defense, and a direction, that the choleric man who reads it will never forget. Why, asks that princely teacher—why has God, who is goodness and love, and who has made man in His own image of goodness and love, why has He kindled in man the choleric temperament? Why has He laid in man's soul, ready for the match, the fires of anger, and resentment, and retaliation, and revenge? And Butler answers his own difficulties as he only can answer them. Anger, he boldly answers, is a sharp sword put into our hand by Nature herself, and she does not intend that that sharp sword should rust in its scabbard. So long as there are evildoers abroad in the earth; so long as injustice, and cruelty, and wrong are inflicted by bad men on their weak and innocent neighbors, so long will God be amply justified for having kindled the sudden fire of anger in good men's hearts, as also for having banked up righteous resentment and recompense against the unjust and wicked man.

But take this temperament as a sound state of the soul; take it as having seated itself in an honest and good heart; and then this temperament of choler and hot coals is surely the very noblest and the very best temperament of all the four. Take a man who has been made a partaker of the divine nature, and put choler into that man's heart, and you have the best manner of man that walks this earth. You have a true nobleman; you have a true prince and a leader of men; you have a true king of men. And all men see him, feel his presence among them, and confess his greatness; for he is open, and free, and hospitable, and full of heart. He is alive where all other men around him are dead. He is bold, brave, fearless, single-eyed, single-hearted, wholehearted, pure-hearted. Where other men wait, and hearken, and hold in, and hesitate, and hedge, and calculate; where other men trim, and steer, and hug the shore; with an eagle eye, with an angel eye, with a divine eye, he sees the right way afar off, and is already far on in it. Opposition, resistance, suffering even, do not alter his mind nor shake his heart, unless it be still more to purify his mind and his heart, and still more to fix and settle him in the clear and sure way of truth and goodness and love. When you cast stones and discharge weapons at the man whose whole life condemns you, "So help me God," he answers, "here God has set me. Here I stand, if I stand alone." The man with this heat in his heart has the Son of God Himself for his example; for His disciples remembered that it was written of Him, "The zeal of thine house hath eaten me up."

The bad side of this temperament is naked enough and open enough to all. The whole world is full of the woe that the choleric temperament works when it is allowed to become bitter anger, soaking malice, and diabolical revenge. Nations, churches, congregations, families, and the homes and the hearts of men, lie in ashes all around us because of anger and ill-temper. All our other evil passions, taken together, slay their thousands, but this evil passion of anger its tens of thousands. There is always someone in every house—it is a happy house where there are not two—hot as gunpowder. The least thing—in his own house—makes the choleric man a madman. A child's cry will do it at one time, and the same child's laugh at another time; a servant's stumble, a wife's oversight and absence of mind, a chair or a table an inch out of its place, a message not delivered and answered to the imperious and exacting moment, anything, nothing. Like the legendary white thorn of Judea, the choleric man's heart will kindle a conflagration merely by chafing against itself. And then a hot look is darted, a hot word is spoken, a hot blow is dealt; and that house, that home of husband and wife and child, is never the same again as long as one stone of it stands upon another. And then, far worse than even that, there are the covered-up, but hell-hot, ashes of ill-will and malice and hatred. "Gunpowder," says an old author, "will take and will fall into a blaze sooner than lime, and yet lime hath the more hidden and scathing heat; it burns far longer, and far more inwardly; and if you put your hand or your foot inadvertently into it, it burns far more deadly." It is Paul's fear lest their sudden anger should smolder down into lifelong hatred that makes the Apostle beseech all his readers not to let the sun go down upon their wrath. Jeremy Taylor, in his rich commentary on the Sixth Commandment, tells us an ancient story or two, as his delightful manner is. Leontius Patricius was one day extremely angry with John, the patriarch of Alexandria; but one evening the patriarch sent this message to the angry man, "Sir, the sun is set." On which, Patricius, being a reader of Paul, took the hint, threw away his anger, and became wholly subject to the counsel and the ghostly aids of the patriarch. And, again, Plutarch, the prince of storytellers, and the source of Taylor's best stories, reports to us that the Pythagoreans were such strict observers of the very letter of this caution that at sunset they always shook hands and departed home friends.

But by far the most deceitful and destructive kind of choler is choler for God. There are many men among us who would see at once that it had its rise in their own evil hearts if they were plunged into anger at wife or child or servant or dog or horse or chair or table, who are as angry as hell itself on account of religion, and all the time think that they do God an acceptable service. Even Moses, who, up to that day, seemed to have been born without bile altogether, even Moses, the meekest of men, fell, for God's sake, into an unpardonable sin. For one hot word against his erring brethren, for one hot stroke of his staff against the unoffending rock, Moses lived all his after days under a cloud, and so died. And, in times of religious controversy, our very best men say and do the most rancorous things, nurse and feed their own and other people's bad passions, hate men, and hate even the fathers and mothers and wives and children of men who, in a few years, are admitted by the whole world to have been right. Just think of a saint like Lord Shaftesbury speaking of a book he did not like as having been spewed out of hell—the most beautiful book on the life of our Lord that ever was written. Of all kinds of choler, let all earnest and God-fearing men watch and beware of religious choler. The *odium theologicum* is the devil's hottest, most deceitful, and most deadly coal.

That man, says Jacob Behmen, who has his soul compassed about with a choleric complexion must, above all things, practice at every turn, and exercise himself like an athlete, in humility. He must every day pour the cold water of humility on the hot coals of his own complexion. Therefore, exclaims Teutonicus, thou that art choleric, take warning and advice. Be a humble-minded man. Press with all thy might after meekness in word and thought; and so shall not thy temperament enflame thy soul. Thy temperament is not alien to God; only take good care of its evil tendency and temptations. Choleric man, mortify thy temperament and thy complexion. And do it all to the glory of God.

Another good thing to do is this. Say every day to yourself that you know yourself. Say to yourself that you have good cause to know yourself. Say how much you have suffered from yourself. And admit also and confess how much other people, and especially your own people, have suffered from you. Say to yourself that you know now, what all men have long known, that you are a very choleric and a very dangerous man. As often as you see the word "temperament," or "complexion," or "humor," or "passion," in print, or hear any of those words spoken, take occasion to tell yourself on the spot what your peculiar temperament, complexion, humor, ruling passion still is. Never see gunpowder without spiritualizing it. Never see lime without taking it home. Never see fire without pouring water on your own. Never see smoke without a prayer that the fire may not spread.

Then, again, descend to particulars. Stamp out every spark, and pour water on every single cinder in your heart. Tie up your tongue and your hands in the places and beside the people where you are tempted to lash out with the one and to strike out with the other. If you are a father, or a master, or a schoolmaster, or a minister, set a watch on the door of your lips every morning before you encounter the stupid, and the disobedient, and the injurious, and the ungrateful. If you are a public man, and if your duty leads you into places of debate and contention and division, hold your peace. Keep quiet, even if you should burst. Your silence will be your best speech. Everybody knows your mind. The cause will lose nothing, and you will gain much, both for the cause and for yourself, by keeping a watch on the door of your far too choleric mouth. Best of all, be angry, and sin not. But that attainment comes to you only after a long life of banking up your inward fires, making them burn low, and putting them out.

This is the choleric man's prayer out of the *Golden Grove*: Lord, let me be ever courteous, and easy to be entreated. Never let me fall into a peevish or contentious spirit. Let me follow peace with all men, offering forgiveness, inviting them by courtesies, ready to confess my own errors, apt to make amends, and desirous to be reconciled. Give me the spirit of a Christian, charitable, humble, merciful and meek, useful and liberal, angry at nothing but my own sins, and grieving for the sins of others, that, while my passion obeys my reason, and my reason is religious, and my religion is pure and undefiled, managed with humility, and adorned with charity, I may escape Thy anger, which I have deserved, and may dwell in Thy love, and be Thy son and servant forever, through Jesus Christ our Lord. Amen.

The Phlegmatic Temperament

THERE IS some confusion about the derivation and transmission of the epithet "phlegmatic," but the phlegmatic temperament is quite well known to us.

To begin with, the man of a phlegmatic temperament has escaped already all the peculiar temptations of the too sanguine man and the too choleric man. The phlegmatic man has not their hot heart in his bosom. Their hot blood does not roar in his veins. The storms of all kinds of passion that are continually surging and bursting out in them are a mystery to him. They look like wild beasts to him when their passions are on them. Now, that of itself is a great gain to the phlegmatic man. For the man of a hot heart often ruins himself past all recovery before he is a man. He has not seldom sold himself for nought before he knows what he is doing. He has run himself on a hundred rocks, and all his days his prayers and his praises are full of nothing but his broken bones. But the calm, cool, cold man escapes all that. He is not tossed about with every wind. His feet are not on the soft sand. He has his root in himself. He is a solid, stable, strong man. That is, when his phlegmatic temperament is not wholly given over to itself, but is balanced and redressed by its complementary and compensatory virtues.

His enemies call the phlegmatic man unconcerned and indifferent, and so, perhaps, he sometimes is—too much. But even his unconcern, which angers you so much, has its good side. For, if he is unconcerned, then he is unconcerned. He says to himself that your affairs are no concern of his. If he is not busy, he is not busy in other men's matters, not even in yours. He has forgotten, he neither knows, nor cares to know, the things that so much interest so many other people in you. For the life of him, he had forgotten that there ever was a skeleton in your closet. When they ask him, he has forgotten again how old you are. He has been told, Oh, my dear, you know how often I have told you; but, with all that, he has clean forgotten how much you got with your wife. The wearisome, careless man has no idea how many children you have, nor who their mothers were —the first wife or the second. You must not ask him. He has no head. He has no interest. He is all out in the facts of life. He is not a companionable man. He is a most uninteresting man, he has no talk, he knows nothing, no, either about your neighbors to you, or about you to your neighbors. Phlegm has two sides.

Lotze is particularly lenient to the phlegmatic temperament. "I shall perhaps be regarded," he says, "as the advocate of a strange thesis when I say that I regard this temperament as the natural and proper temperament of advanced age, and, at the same time, as an improvement on the choleric temperament, with its prejudices and its narrowness." All true. But, then, this is not the natural temper of advanced age only; it is the natural temper of all ages that are advancing in truth and in goodness; it is the natural temper of all ages in which men are learning to take home to themselves the mischiefs that heat and hurry work, and to lay to heart the great need there is for sobermindedness and self-command, foresight and forethought, among the tempests and whirlpools of human passion. Alas that all our lives should be so far advanced before we come, by sound judgment and a well garnered experience, to the full fruits of our several temperaments. Reason, religion, and growth in character, should achieve for us that balance, and that weight, and that possession and reserve of power over ourselves and over our circumstances which no temperament, the best, will of itself alone give; but to all which this temperament now before us is well fitted to make a large and an immediate contribution. Then, again, just as advancing age gives a man an easy mastery over the rampant passions of his youth, so does this temperament go to help even a young man to that mastery, if he cares to have it. The chorus at the end of *Samson Agonistes* testifies in noble language to that "calm of mind, all passion spent," to which the Highest Wisdom leads all His children at the last, and His children of this temperament soonest and easiest of all.

Sloth sums up, in one short and expressive word, the bad side of this temperament. Some part of what we call sloth in some men is, no doubt, in fairness to be set down to such a phlegmatic constitution that it would take the will and the energy of a giant to overcome it. There are men of such a slow-working heart, their blood creeps through their veins at such a snail's pace, their joints are so loosely knit, and their whole body is so lethargic, that both God and man must take all that into consideration before they condemn them. And when we must say sloth in his case, we still take into account all that can be said in extenuation, and the phlegmatic man will not be blamed for what he could not help. He will be blamed and chastised only for what he could quite well have helped if only he had resolved to help it. At the same time, sloth is sloth, laziness is laziness, whatever your temperament may be. Laziness, indeed, is not of the body at all; it is of the mind, it is of the will, it is of the heart, it is of the moral character. It is not their temperaments that make shipwrecks of so many of our students' and of our ministers' lives. The phlegmatic minister has not worked harder on Sabbath than some of his people have worked every day all the week. But he is a minister, and he has no master beside him but his own conscience, and so he spends all Monday on the sofa with a newspaper and a novel. He will read for his pulpit tomorrow forenoon, and visit his sick in the afternoon. But tomorrow he is not very well in the morning, and it rains in the afternoon. On Wednesday he still has four whole days before Sabbath, and, besides, his letters are in terrible arrears, he has not had time to answer a note for a fortnight. A friend drops in to spend Thursday with him, but what of that? He has all Friday and Saturday to be kept shut up and absolutely sacred. On Friday forenoon he is told that his old elder, who was so ill, is dead, and he is as unhappy a man all that day as you could wish him to be. And he has a very unhappy errand before him that afternoon in having to explain to the bereaved family how busy he was all the beginning of the week. He sits into Saturday morning seeking for his Sabbath text, but has to go to bed before he has found it. All Saturday he has his meals at his desk, and he is like a bear robbed of her whelps if anybody but looks at him or speaks to him. On Sabbath morning he takes an old rag out of his drawer, and his people look at one another, as he cannot even read it. Brother minister, of the most remote and illiterate congregation in Scotland, sit down to thy desk early every day, and if God has made thee of a slothful, lethargic, phlegmatic temperament, only sit down all the more doggedly. Let every lazy student of divinity, and with him every waiting, complaining, postponing probationer, go drown himself at once.

The phlegmatic temperament has its compensations at some times, in some companies, and in some circumstances, but never in the study, and, of all the places on the earth, never in the closet. Fight with thy worst devil, thy slothful self, in thy place of secret prayer every day and every night. Thy battle is set thee there. It is set thee there by the Captain of thy salvation, whose zeal ate Him up day and night. Thy crown will be won by thee or taken from thee there. Fight the good fight with thy phlegmatic temperament there. Fight with thy constitutional sloth there. Fight this day with thy procrastination there. Blot out tomorrow there.